DISCLAIMER

This book provides general informational advice and is not intended to replace professional advice. The author and publisher disclaim any liability for any errors or omissions in the content.

Readers are advised to exercise caution when applying the suggestions, as individual circumstances vary. Before making significant lifestyle changes or adopting new health practices, it is strongly advised to consult with qualified professionals, such as healthcare practitioners or nutritionists, to ensure the recommendations are safe and suitable for their specific situation.

The author and publisher are not responsible for any misuse, misunderstanding, or misinterpretation of the content and are not liable for any consequences arising from their use.

The book also emphasizes the importance of a holistic health approach, which should be undertaken under the guidance of experts to maximize effectiveness and safety. Individuals with existing health conditions or those taking medication should consult with their healthcare providers before making significant changes to their lifestyle, diet, or health practices.

An Overview of the Universal Cosmic Energy Effect and its Implications on Human Existence

saptagyanam

CONCEPTUALIZED BY: **Ar. K. SHIVKUMAR**

An Approach To
"PGR" Measures
(Preventive, Guiding & Remedial)

"These 'SAPTAGYANAM' Approaches explains the secret of how to open oneself up to the Natural Cosmic Energies around us,

how to sensitize oneself to them and

how to use our Natural Instincts and Intuition to our last limit".

INDIA • SINGAPORE • MALAYSIA

INTRODUCTION

My inclined interest and fundamental knowledge of above areas accompanied with the hardcore experience related to safeguarding one's health during the on-going worldwide Covid-19 pandemic crises, enforced me to conceptualize the book 'SAPTAMSIDHI' dealing on varied Holistic Health approaches in sync with the Indian Vedic Culture and its impact and relevance in today's modern lifestyle. 'SAPTAMSIDHI' – being the principally conceptualized book, followed by other additional titles **"SAPTAGYANAM"**, SANSKAARAM, PRANOYUGAM & AAROGYAVEDA.

SAPTAGYANAM being one among the other 4 more additional tiles of 'SAPTAMSIDHI, introduces the reader about the UNIVERSAL HOLISTIC HEALTH APPROACHES practiced worldwide through ages as alternate remedial measures for minimizing the cause and the effects of the various Natural Energies of this Cosmic, directly impacting human beings on this mother "EARTH".

It provides an insight to **"WELL-BEING"** mantra in terms of natural healing faculties through **(The PGR Measures)** – **The Preventive, Guiding & Remedial Measures** caused by the time and effect of planetary movements and environmental factors effecting throughout our life.

The '7' – Introductory Topics are thought-full study contents, unfolding curiosities and interpretation leading to conclusions. These are conceptualized in such a manner that it influences and convince the reader to create an optimal level of awareness to environmentally adapt and practically accept the underlined principles of **Indian Vedic Culture** in accordance with the **Universal Natural Phenomenon and its Energy**, focusing our mind on analytical inquiries and therapeutic outcomes.

Tabulated Formats (TF) are condensed contents in table form that give the reader with the whole summary and highlighted significant points of each chapter at a glance on a single page.

Each chapter has a plethora of photographs, diagrams, and visual interpretations to provide a clear and concise grasp of the underlying subject matter.

The information described, evaluated, and presented as an instant ready reckoner for all age groups can be used at various points throughout one's life.

FOREWORD

BANARAS HINDU
UNIVERSITY

Established by The BANARAS HINDU UNIVERSITY ACT XVI of 1915

IMBHU
प्रबंध शास्त्र संकाय
FACULTY OF MANAGEMENT STUDIES
INSTITUTE OF MANAGEMENT STUDIES

Date: 07-01-2024

FOREWORD

It gives me immense pleasure to know that **Architect K. Shivkumar** has conceptualised the book titled **"SAPTAMSIDHI"**– the Principle book which is followed by its other supplementary titles 'SANSKAARAM', 'PRANOYUGAM', 'AAROGYAVEDA' & 'SAPTAGYANAM'.

The author has made a singular attempt in providing readers with a Reference Handbook for Wellness & Wellbeing that blends Ancient Practical Vedic Approaches for Today's Modern Lifestyle with advice on how to protect oneself from Modern Lifestyle Disorders through Prevention, Screening, and Treatment Measures.

Globally, there is an upsurge in psychiatric and lifestyle illnesses. I believe that these described and applied unique Vedic approaches and selected Yoga techniques such as Asanas, Pranayama, Mantras, Meditation, Mudras, and so on, when combined with the '7'- Seven different types of Holistic Health Approaches in sync with Indian Vedic culture, will provide a Holistic Treatment to cure these Modern Lifestyle Disorders miraculously.

This book's content will undoubtedly empower readers with a ready grasp of Hindu philosophy and profound information, helping them to live a healthier, happier, and stress-free life.

I truly think that **Architect K. Shivkumar's** book will be of great assistance to human society worldwide, and I applaud his efforts in creating an insightful and instructive work.

Prof. H. P. Mathur,
B.Tech. (IT-BHU), MMS, CAIIB, Ph.D.
Dean & Head,
Faculty of Management Studies, BHU.

Chairman, FMS/IM, BHU Placement Cell.
Director, Atal Incubation Centre, IM, BHU.
Director, Utkarsh Welfare Foundation.
Member, Board of Governors, UPES University.
Former Chief, University Employment Info & Guidance Bureau, BHU.
Former Coordinator, BHU Placement Coordination Cell.
Former Chairman, International Centre, BHU.

CONTENTS

Contents

VI. NUMEROLOGY

VII. CHROMOTHERAPY

*An Introduction to the 'SEVEN' aspects of Inter-related Cosmic
Energy & it's Impact on Human Existence.*

VAASTUTATVAH

1. **VAASTU SHASTRA**
   a. *DEFINING VAASTU SHASTRA*
      - Meaning, Interpretation & Application of Vaastu Shastra
      - Components of Vaastu Shastra
   b. *RELATION WITH PANCHATATVAS*
      - Interpretation of Panchatatvas in Vaastu Shastra
      - Relevance of Panchatatvas in Vaastu Shastra
   c. *IMPORTANCE OF VAASTU PURUSH MANDALA*
      - Pictorial explanation of Vaastu Purush Mandala
      - Importance of Vaastu Purush Mandala
      - The presiding deities of each direction
   d. *TIPS FOR WELLNESS & WELLBEING AS PER VAASTU SHASTRA*

2. **ROLE OF ENERGY IN VAASTU SHASTRA –** (**'Pranic, Jaivic & Solar Energy'**)
   - Interpretation of Pranic, Jaivic & Solar Energy in context to Vaastu Shastra
   - Role of Pranic, Jaivic & Solar Energy in Vaastu Shastra
   - FAQ's

3. **VAASTU SHASTRA & ASTROLOGY**

4. **VAASTU SHASTRA & NUMEROLOGY**
   - Relation between Vaastu Shastra & Numerology
   - Relevance of Numerology in Vaastu Shastra
   - The Calculation and Table form – corelating Numerology & Vaastu Shastra

5. **VAASTU SHASTRA & COLOR THERAPY**
   - Relation between Vaastu Shastra & Chromotherapy
   - Colors and their meaning as per Vaastu Shastra
   - Impact of Vaastu colors and its relevance in a Residential House.

6. **VAASTU TIPS FOR RESIDENTIAL, OFFICIAL, COMMERCIAL & INDUSTRIAL SPACES**
   - House Vaastu
   - Office Vaastu
   - Shop Vaastu
   - Industry / Factory Vaastu

7. **VAASTUTATVAH & ITS VARIOUS ASPECTS w.r.t – 8 DIRECTIONS & BRAHMASTHAN – (TF)**

AN INTRODUCTION TO VAASTU SHASTRA IN VEDIC CONTEXT

Vaastu Shastra, often referred to simply as Vaastu, is an ancient Indian Architectural and Design philosophy that has its roots in the Vedic tradition. This time-honoured discipline is deeply intertwined with the spiritual and philosophical aspects of Vedic culture, and it seeks to create harmonious and balanced living spaces by adhering to a set of principles derived from Vedic texts.

The term "Vaastu" is derived from the Sanskrit words "Vas," which means "to dwell," and "Shastra," which means "knowledge" or "science." Therefore, Vaastu Shastra can be translated as the "science of dwelling" or **"the Science of Architecture."** It is a comprehensive system that provides guidelines for constructing and arranging homes, temples, and other structures in a manner that promotes positive energy flow and well-being for the occupants.

Vaastu Shastra is believed to have its origins in texts like the Vedas and Upanishads, which are foundational scriptures of Vedic wisdom. The principles of Vaastu are based on the idea that the universe is interconnected, and the alignment and design of a physical space can influence the flow of cosmic energy and, consequently, the quality of life within that space.

In Vedic context, Vaastu Shastra is considered a holistic approach to architecture and design, focusing on not only the physical and aesthetic aspects of a building but also its spiritual and cosmic significance. It takes into account the position of the sun, moon, and stars, as well as the five elements—earth, water, fire, air, and space – to create spaces that resonate with the natural order of the universe.

The fundamental aim of Vaastu Shastra is to create an environment that promotes health, prosperity, and spiritual growth while minimizing negative influences and spaces that are not only aesthetically pleasing but also conducive to overall well-being.

1

VAASTU SHASTRA

A) DEFINING VAASTU SHASTRA

MEANING, INTERPRETATION & APPLICATION OF VAASTU SHASTRA

Vedic Vaastu Shastra is an ancient Indian science of architecture that originated from the Vedas, the ancient sacred texts of India. It provides guidelines and principles for designing and constructing buildings or spaces in harmony with nature, the environment, and cosmic energies.

1. **Meaning:**
   - **Vedic:** Vedic Vaastu Shastra is rooted in the Vedic tradition, which is one of the oldest known scriptures in Hinduism.
   - **Vaastu:** The term "Vaastu" refers to the dwelling or building, and "Shastra" means knowledge or science. So, Vaastu Shastra is the science of creating harmonious living spaces.

2. **Interpretation:**
   - **Cosmic Harmony:** Vedic Vaastu Shastra believes that every living being and object in the universe is interconnected and influenced by cosmic energies. It aims to create a harmonious and balanced living environment that aligns with the natural forces.

- **Five Elements:** The foundation of Vedic Vaastu lies in the understanding and balance of the five elements – Earth, Water, Fire, Air, and Space termed as Panchatatvas. Each element is associated with specific directions and energies.
- **Energy Flow:** Vedic Vaastu emphasizes the flow of energy (Prana) in a space and how it can affect the physical, mental, and spiritual well-being of the occupants. The goal is to enhance the positive energy flow and minimize negative influences.

3. **Application:**
   - **Site Selection:** Vedic Vaastu begins with the selection of an auspicious site for construction. Factors such as the direction, slope, shape, and surroundings of the plot are considered to determine its energy suitability.
   - **Layout and Design:** The layout and design of the building are based on the principles of the Vaastu Purush Mandala, a grid representing the cosmic energies and the Vaastu Purush. Proper orientation of rooms and placement of elements aim to optimize energy flow.
   - **Directional Influences:** Each direction is associated with specific energies and elements. For example, the North is associated with wealth and prosperity, while the East is connected to new beginnings. Vedic Vaastu considers these directional influences in designing various spaces.

- **Elemental Balancing:** Vedic Vaastu seeks to balance the five elements within a structure, ensuring that no element dominates or is lacking. This balance is achieved through the proper placement of elements, colours, and materials.
- **Rituals and Blessings:** Before starting construction, certain rituals and ceremonies may be performed to seek blessings and consent from the Vaastu Purush and the deities associated with the site.

Vedic Vaastu Shastra is a holistic approach to architecture that incorporates the art and science of designing living spaces to promote harmony, prosperity, and well-being. While some principles of Vedic Vaastu Shastra may align with modern architectural and design practices, its spiritual and metaphysical aspects make it unique in its approach. It continues to be practiced and respected by many to this day as a way to create living environments that are in sync with the natural and cosmic energies.

COMPONENTS OF VASTU SHASTRA

Vaastu Shastra, the ancient Indian science of architecture, consists of several components that collectively guide the design, layout, and construction of living and working spaces. These components are based on the principles of cosmic energy, the five elements (Panchatatva), and the interplay between human beings and their environment. Here are the main components of Vaastu Shastra:

What is Vastushastra....?

- 8 Directions
- 5 Elements
- Gravitational & Electro Magnetic force of Earth.
- Cosmic Waves
- Enrich human life.

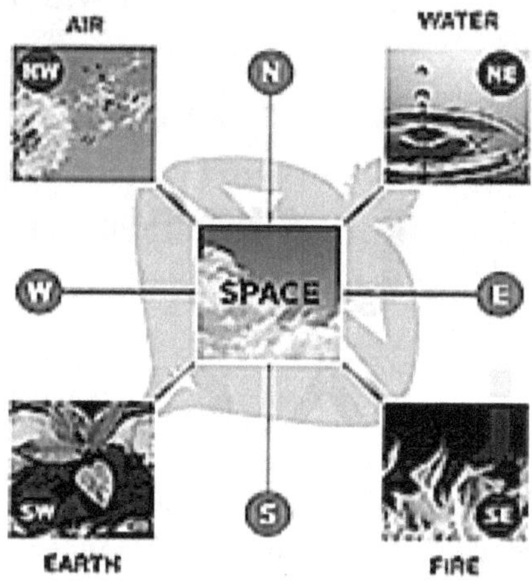

1. **Directions (Dikpala):** Vaastu Shastra places great emphasis on the cardinal directions – North, South, East, West, as well as the four intermediate directions – Northeast, Southeast, Southwest, and Northwest. Each direction is associated with specific energies and elements, and the proper orientation of a building or space is determined by these directions.

2. **Five Elements (Panchatatva):** The foundation of Vaastu Shastra lies in the understanding and balance of the five elements – Earth (Prithvi), Water (Ap/Jal), Fire (Tejas), Air (Vayu), and Space (Akasha). Each element is linked to specific directions and energies, and their balance is essential for a harmonious living space.

3. **Vaastu Purush Mandala:** The Vaastu Purush Mandala is a symbolic representation of the cosmic energies and the Vaastu Purush, a deity embodying the spirit of the space.

It is a grid used to determine the proper placement of rooms and elements within a building based on their association with the energies of different directions.

4. **Zoning and Layout:** Vaastu Shastra provides guidelines for the zoning and layout of different spaces within a building or plot. The arrangement of rooms, entrances, and common areas is based on the principles of energy flow and elemental balance.

5. **Main Entrance (Mukha dwar):** The main entrance of a building is a crucial component of Vaastu Shastra. It is considered the gateway for energy and should be positioned in a favourable direction to attract positive energy.

6. **Rooms and Their Placements:** Vaastu Shastra prescribes the ideal locations for specific rooms based on their purpose and association with certain energies. For example, the kitchen is best placed in the Southeast direction, while the bedroom is recommended in the Southwest direction.

7. **Colours and Materials:** The choice of colours and building materials is an integral part of Vaastu Shastra. Colours are associated with specific energies, and the use of natural materials is encouraged to create a positive and harmonious environment.

8. **Proportions and Measurements:** Vaastu Shastra considers the proportions and measurements of a building to ensure aesthetic and energetic balance. Certain ratios, such as the Golden Ratio, may be used in architectural design.

9. **Vaastu Remedies:** For existing structures that do not conform to Vaastu principles, there are remedies that can be applied to mitigate negative energies and bring positive changes.

These components collectively form the framework of Vaastu Shastra, guiding architects, builders, and homeowners in creating spaces that are in harmony with nature and promote well-being and prosperity for the occupants. While adhering strictly to all Vaastu principles may not always be practical, integrating some aspects of Vaastu Shastra can contribute to creating a balanced and positive living environment.

B) RELATION WITH PANCHATATVAS

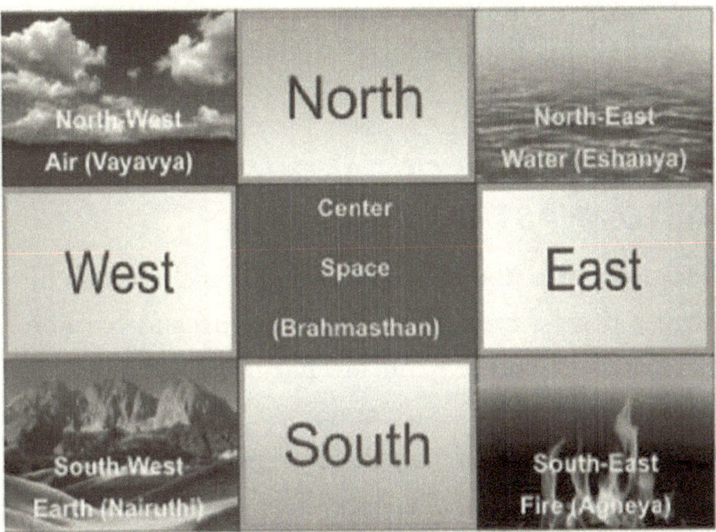

Our ancient saints have concluded that anything living or non-living in the universe is made up of five basic elements or **PANCHAMAHABUTAS / PANCHATATVAS**. Vaastu is directly related to these five elements which are as follows:

	ELEMENT		FORM OF ENERGY
1.	**PRITHVI –**	(Earth)	GRAVITATIONAL / MAGNETIC
2.	**JAL –**	(Water)	RAIN
3.	**AGNI –**	(Fire)	SOLAR
4.	**VAYU –**	(Air)	WIND
5.	**AAKASH –**	(Space)	SOUND

1. The magnetic field, gravitational effect etc. of Earth.
2. The volume and intensity of rainfall and source of Water inside our Mother Earth etc.
3. Light and Heat of the Sun including the effects of its Ultra-Violet and Infra-Red rays.

4. The direction and velocity of the wind and seasonal changes of our world.

5. The Galaxy in the sky, stars and planets around the Earth and their effects.

INTERPRETATION OF PANCHATATVA IN VAASTU SHASTRA

In Vaastu Shastra, the interpretation of Panchatatvas (the five elements) plays a crucial role in designing and harmonizing living spaces. These elements are Earth (Prithvi), Water (Ap/Jal), Fire (Tejas), Air (Vayu), and Space (Akasha). The proper balance and alignment of these elements are believed to create a harmonious and energetically positive environment. Here's the interpretation of Panchatatvas in Vaastu Shastra:

1. **Earth (Prithvi):**
   - **Direction:** Southwest
   - **Significance:** Earth element represents stability, grounding, and nourishment. It provides a sense of security and support.
   - **Interpretation:** The southwest area of a building is ideally suited for heavy structures, master bedrooms, and storage spaces. It's associated with stability, wealth accumulation, and a sense of security.

2. **Water (Ap/Jal):**
   - **Direction:** Northeast
   - **Significance:** Water symbolizes fluidity, emotional well-being, and purity. It represents the flow of energy and life.

- **Interpretation:** The northeast corner is suitable for water-related elements like water storage, fountains, or small water bodies. It enhances positive energies, promotes clarity, and supports spiritual growth.

3. **Fire (Tejas):**
   - **Direction:** Southeast
   - **Significance:** Fire embodies transformation, energy, and warmth. It represents the vitality and inspiration in life.
   - **Interpretation:** The southeast area is conducive to placing the kitchen, electrical appliances, and heat-related elements. It fosters dynamic energy, creativity, and enhances the health and vitality of the occupants.

4. **Air (Vayu):**
   - **Direction:** Northwest
   - **Significance:** Air signifies movement, communication, and change. It represents openness and freshness.
   - **Interpretation:** The northwest corner is suitable for airy and light structures. Placing living rooms or common areas here can encourage social interactions, networking, and adaptability.

5. **Space (Akasha):**
   - **Direction:** Center
   - **Significance:** Space represents the infinite, boundless potential, and the unmanifested. It's the canvas upon which the other elements interact.
   - **Interpretation:** The centre of a building should be kept open, clutter-free, and well-ventilated. This

area promotes balance, harmony, and serves as a pivot around which other energies revolve.

The interpretation of Panchatatvas in Vaastu Shastra involves understanding the attributes of each element, their associated directions, and their influence on human life and well-being. The goal is to create a harmonious alignment of these elements within the living space, which is believed to foster positive energies, balance, and overall prosperity. It's important to note that while adhering to these principles can be beneficial, practicality and individual circumstances should also be considered when implementing Vaastu guidelines.

RELEVANCE OF PANCHATATVAS IN VAASTU SHASTRA

The Panchatatvas, or the five elements, play a central and crucial role in Vaastu Shastra. These principles of Panchatatvas are deeply embedded in the design, layout, and construction of buildings to create a harmonious and balanced living environment. The relevance of Panchatatvas in Vaastu Shastra can be understood through the following points:

1. **Balancing Energies:** The Panchatatvas represent the five fundamental energies that make up the universe. In Vaastu Shastra, the proper balance and alignment of these energies within a living space are believed to contribute to the well-being and prosperity of the occupants.

2. **Directions and Elements:** Each of the five elements is associated with specific cardinal and intermediate directions. For example, Earth is associated with the

Southwest, Water with the Northeast, Fire with the Southeast, Air with the Northwest, and Space with the Centre. The correct placement of rooms and elements based on their associated elements and directions is a key aspect of Vaastu design.

3. **Energy Flow:** The proper alignment of the elements in a building allows for smooth energy flow throughout the space. It is believed that this balanced flow of energies enhances positive vibrations and promotes good health, happiness, and success.

4. **Cosmic Harmony:** Vaastu Shastra seeks to align the human living space with the cosmic energies. By incorporating the elements in the design, the architecture aims to create a harmonious connection with the broader universe.

5. **Auspiciousness and Purification:** The Panchatatvas are considered sacred and symbolize purity. By incorporating the elements into the design and decor, Vaastu aims to create a pure and auspicious environment that promotes spiritual well-being.

6. **Elemental Remedies:** In Vaastu Shastra, specific remedies and enhancements based on the Panchatatvas are used to correct imbalances or negative influences in a living space. For instance, the use of certain colours, materials, or natural elements can be employed as remedies to improve the overall energy of the space.

7. **Environmental Balance:** Vaastu Shastra emphasizes the need to create an environment that is in harmony with nature. By incorporating the five elements, the design

can be aligned with the natural elements present in the surroundings.

8. **Holistic Approach:** The incorporation of the Panchatatvas in Vaastu design ensures a holistic approach to living spaces. It takes into consideration not only the physical aspects of the building but also its energetic and spiritual aspects.

In summary, the Panchatatvas are the fundamental building blocks of Vaastu Shastra, and their proper balance and integration in the design of living spaces are believed to create a positive, harmonious, and spiritually uplifting environment for the occupants

C) IMPORTANCE OF VAASTU PURUSH MANDALA

The God of structures, also known as – **Vaastu Purush**, provides protection, happiness and prosperity to its habitants if Vaastu principles are followed.

PICTORIAL EXPLANATION OF VAASTU PURUSH MANDALA

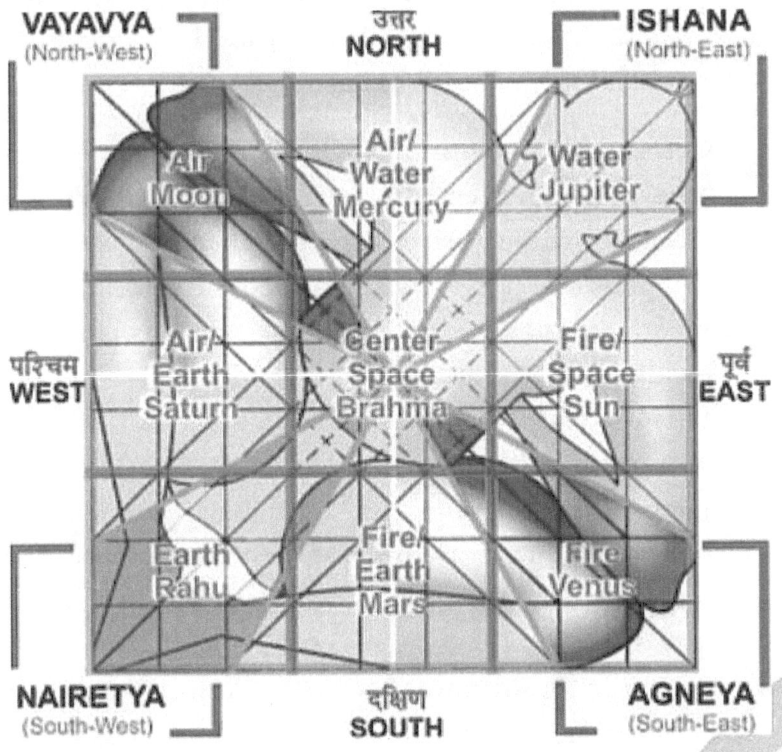

[*MANDALA* – *It is a collective name for a chart or a plan that symbolically represents the UNIVERSE and PURUSHA – indicates to a cosmic man, energy connection, power or soul.*

The Vaastu Purusha Mandala is metaphysical planning of building that subsumes (include or absorb) the journey of supernatural forces and heavenly bodies – (COSMIC ENERGY)].

IMPORTANCE OF VAASTU PURUSH MANDALA

Vaastu Purush Mandala is a crucial concept in Vaastu Shastra. It plays a fundamental role in determining the energy flow and spatial arrangement of a building or plot. The Vaastu Purush Mandala is a symbolic representation of the cosmic energy and the universal spirit that governs a space. Let's explore the importance of Vaastu Purush Mandala:

1. **Cosmic Alignment:** The Vaastu Purush Mandala is believed to represent the body of the Vaastu Purush, a deity or cosmic being who embodies the energies of the universe. It symbolizes the cosmic alignment of energy and the connection between the microcosm (the building) and the macrocosm (the universe).

2. **Energy Grid:** The Mandala is a grid with different divisions and directions that allocate specific deities and energies to different parts of a building. Each direction is associated with a particular element and planetary energy, and it helps in balancing and channelling the flow of energy within the structure.

3. **Symbolic Significance:** The Vaastu Purush Mandala is a sacred and revered symbol in Vaastu Shastra. It represents the harmonious coexistence of various energies, deities, and forces that influence the living or working space.

4. **Spatial Arrangement:** The Mandala provides guidelines for the spatial arrangement of rooms and zones within a

building. It helps in deciding the placement of the main entrance, the kitchen, bedrooms, and other rooms based on the energies associated with different directions.

5. **Energy Balance:** The arrangement of spaces within the Vaastu Purush Mandala aims to achieve a balance of the five elements (Panchatatva) – Earth, Water, Fire, Air, and Space. This balance is thought to bring harmony and positive vibrations to the inhabitants.

6. **Positive Influence:** It is believed that aligning the design of a building or plot with the Vaastu Purush Mandala can have a positive influence on the well-being, health, prosperity, and overall happiness of the occupants.

7. **Sacred Rituals:** Before commencing construction on a site, traditional Vaastu practices often involve performing rituals and seeking blessings from the Vaastu Purush as a way to seek his consent and divine guidance for the project.

8. **Architectural Symbolism:** The Vaastu Purush Mandala serves as a symbolic representation of the underlying philosophy and spiritual aspects of Vaastu Shastra. It brings a deeper level of meaning and purpose to the architectural design.

In summary, the Vaastu Purush Mandala is a powerful and significant symbol in Vaastu Shastra, reflecting the cosmic connection between the built environment and the universe. By following its principles, architects and homeowners aim to create a harmonious and balanced space that aligns with the natural energies and influences, promoting well-being and prosperity.

The Vaastu Purush Mandala is a specific type of mandala/ grid used in Vaastu Shastra. It is the metaphysical plan of a building / temple / site, that incorporates the course of the heavenly bodies and supernatural forces.

THE PRINCIPAL GODS / PRESIDING DEITIES OF EACH DIRECTION ARE LISTED BELOW

Direction	Ruling God / Deity
North-West (Vayavya)	Ruled by Lord of Winds
North – Kubera	Ruled by Lord of Wealth
North – East (Eashan)	Ruled by Lord of all quarters or Lord Shiva
East	Ruled by God Sun – Aditya (Indra)
South – East (Agni)	Ruled by Lord of Fire – Agni
South – Yama	Ruled by Lord of Death – Yama
South – West (Nairutya)	Pitru / Nairutya, Nairuthi – Ruled by ancestors
West – Varuna	Ruled by Lord of Water
Centre (Brahma)	**Ruled by Lord or Creator of the Universe**

According to Vaastu Shastra, if the house is designed as per Vaastu Purusha Mandala, a perfectly balanced environment is achieved, which ensures enhanced health, wealth and happiness.

The Scientific Explanation: This is actually based on scientific principles wherein, the Sun, the five basic elements (Panchabhutaas), the Earth's magnetic field, the Earth's energy field and the eight directions are manipulated to achieve an optimum level of balance between the Cosmic energies of the universe and the built environment to create an atmosphere beneficial to human beings.

D) TIPS FOR WELLNESS & WELLBEING AS PER VAASTU SHASTRA

Vaastu Shastra, the ancient Indian science of architecture, emphasizes creating a balanced and harmonious living space to enhance overall wellness and well-being. The principles of Vaastu can be applied to create a positive and conducive environment for physical, mental, and spiritual health. Here are some Vaastu tips for wellness and well-being:

1. **Northeast Zone:**
   - The Northeast zone is considered highly auspicious and is associated with positive energies. Keep this area clean, clutter-free, and well-lit.
   - Place a meditation corner or a puja room in the Northeast direction to promote spiritual well-being.

2. **Bedroom:**
   - The bedroom should be in the Southwest or South direction for better rest and sleep. Avoid placing the bed under overhead beams and head pointing the north direction while sleeping.
   - Use calming and soothing colours in the bedroom, such as pastel shades of blue or green.

3. **Kitchen:**
   - The kitchen should be located in the Southeast corner of the house. This direction is associated with the fire element and promotes health and vitality.
   - Ensure that the kitchen is well-ventilated and receives sufficient natural light.

4. **Living Area:**
   - The living room or common area should be in the North or East direction for a positive and vibrant atmosphere.
   - Use bright and cheerful colours in the living area to uplift the mood.

5. **Fresh Air and Natural Light:**
   - Ensure proper ventilation in all rooms to allow fresh air to circulate.
   - Maximize natural light by using large windows and keeping the space uncluttered.

6. **Indoor Plants:**
   - Place indoor plants in the living area and other rooms. They not only purify the air but also add a touch of natural beauty.
   - Avoid keeping thorny or dried plants inside the house.

7. **Water Elements:**
   - A small water fountain or aquarium in the North or East direction can enhance positive energy flow.
   - Avoid placing water elements in the bedroom or the South direction.

8. **Clutter Management:**
   - Keep the living space tidy and clutter-free. Clutter can disrupt the flow of positive energy.
   - Regularly declutter and organize your belongings.

9. **Personal Space:**
   - Dedicate a personal space in the house where you can engage in activities that promote relaxation and well-being, such as reading or yoga.

10. **Electromagnetic Fields (EMFs):**
    - Minimize the use of electronic devices in the bedroom, especially near the bed, as they can disrupt sleep patterns.

Vaastu tips for wellness and well-being are meant to be applied in conjunction with other healthy lifestyle practices. A balanced diet, regular exercise, and stress management are also crucial for overall health and well-being. Consult with a qualified Vaastu expert to customize these tips based on your specific living space and needs.

By following principles of Vaastu Shastra laid down by the ancient Indian scholars, it is possible to prevent mental agony, negative energy, and achieve mental peace. By applying some simple corrective measures, several health problems can be prevented, avoided or remedied.

Here are a few basic pointers of Vaastu to ensure good health and peaceful relationships – Do's & Don'ts to eradicate negative energy and maximise positive energy in a house.

1. Avoid keeping your head towards the north while sleeping; instead, try keeping it towards south or east direction, to achieve peaceful and restful sleep for a healthy life. According to Vaastu, it's important to make sure your bedroom is in the south-west direction.
2. Paint the master bedroom in purple, violet tones to inspire trust.
3. Increase the amount of light that enters the house and keep the house lit at all times, until bed time.

4. Mirrors facing the bed in a bedroom encourage infidelity. Larger the size of the mirror, more harmful it is to a marriage life.

5. Try facing east or north while working, studying or negotiating with clients. It aide's memory, thereby allowing one to take proper timely decisions.

6. Avoid facing south or south-west while cooking, eating or drinking. You should ideally face towards east or west for better taste, digestion & a healthy body.

7. Avoid cooking with your back towards a door. It may lead to backache, pain in the legs, shoulder & fatigue.

8. Planting a few Basil (Tulsi) shrubs in the house helps to purify the air. Avoid plants such as Cactus, Rubber Plants, Milky Plants and Bonsai in the house as they might add to your stress and illness.

9. Stairs, toilets in north-east corner of the property may lead to health-related issues. It can also hamper the growth of small children.

10. Avoid sitting, working, or sleeping under a beam, it may cause headache, inhibit memory, and cause depression.

11. To avoid any health problem related to heart & brain, try using wooden beds without storage space and avoid sleeping on metal beds.

12. Any place that is constantly damp or smells of dampness, with or without the cause being evident or visible, is considered to have or emit negative energy. It is best to avoid such spaces.

13. To minimize disorders related to heart and the nervous system, avoid usage of space below the staircase for

bathroom, toilet, and pantry, or even for closed storage of food grains and eatables.

14. Decorate the house with crystal showpieces and centre pieces. Crystal assists in attracting light, thus lighting up your relationship.

15. De-clutter your living space. Cluttered things tend to restrict the flow of positive energy.

16. Water bodies inside the house should always be placed as per the Vaastu norms. Improper placement can lead to marital issues.

17. Large open spaces in the north attract wealth. So, remove all obstacles and storages from north.

18. Locate the cupboard or safe for keeping cash and jewellery in the south or south-west zone. It should open towards the north, the direction of Kuber. Keep the north-east portion of the house open and free from clutter. Never have a staircase at this location.

19. Make water bodies in the north, underground water tanks can be in this zone, avoid underground tanks in southern zone.

20. Always sit facing north. Make all seating arrangements along the southern and western wall.

21. Never have a dripping faucet or plumbing as it drains the finances of the house.

2

ROLES OF ENERGIES IN VASTU SHASTRA – ('PRANIC', 'JAIVIC' & SOLAR ENERGY)

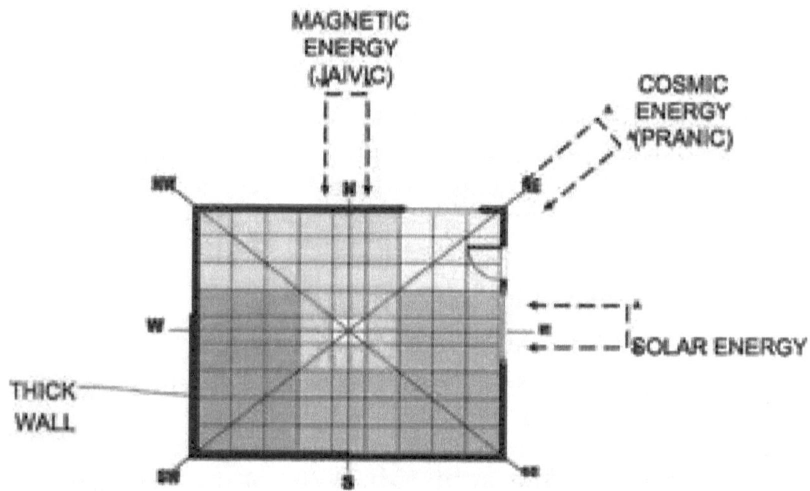

POSITION OF MAGNETIC, COSMIC & SOLAR ENERGY IN VAASTU SHASTRA GRID

I) COSMIC ENERGY ('PRANIC' ENERGY)

As we know our Earth is tilted 23.5 degrees towards the North-East direction and it is moving from West to East direction. For an example, when we run, we feel the air is coming against our direction. We feel the air.

Similar thing happens to the movement of Earth towards the North-East direction vis-à-vis the Cosmic Energy ('Pranic' Energy), which comes in from the North-East direction.

This is the reason that much focus is paid towards the North-East direction. If this zone is blocked then the breadwinner will face many difficulties in life.

No obstruction should be along the North-East zone; like bathroom, toilet, storeroom, staircase, master bedroom or even kitchen should **not** be placed there. Only prayer room is allowed there.

This area must be kept clean and tidy and preferably lightweight or no weight at all. Keep windows open here in the morning for the beneficial morning Sun.

Use this place for meditation and prayers. Preferably face East or West always while praying and the temple/deity position in North-East location of the house. Avoid placing a temple location in the south direction. In addition, keep a bowl of water (clean water) and place it at the corner of the North-East zone.

North-East zone represents the water element in Vaastu. Respect this zone as if it's the heart of the house. This room can be used if you are not well and wish to get well fast and to recharge yourself when you are stressed out.

Why there are some cases of houses being burgled or robbed by thieves while some are not; certain people get robbed; some dogs attack people easily and some dogs don't and keep their distance? This may be connected to the energy level of people and their homes.

When a person's energy level or 'Prana' energy level is low, dogs can sense it and they may attack. If a house energy level is low, thieves might sense it and notice it. How can they sense it?

It comes down to their intuition and instinct and their feeling towards it. That is why that in some houses we sense good vibes and in some, we don't.

II) MAGNETIC FIELD ('JAIVIC' ENERGY)

Magnetic field of Earth flows from North to South. We as humans can only observe this energy when we sleep. If we get bad dreams, cannot sleep at night, or sleeping in excess then we may be or are sleeping with our heads towards North.

Our body is receptive to the North-South Magnetic flow is due to IRON in our blood. Our head reacts as the North Pole and legs as South Pole.

When we sleep with our heads towards North, our head and the North Pole repels each other, and we get disturbed sleep. Sometimes we may even get migraine and headaches sleeping towards this direction.

The best direction to sleep is towards South. When North and South Pole is against each other, it attracts and we get sound and blissful sleep. It is advisable to sleep with our heads pointing towards South, if not possible complete South; it can be South-East or South-West too, but never towards North-East or North-West and North.

III) SOLAR ENERGY

The source of solar energy is only from the Sun. It is the source of Vitamin D as well. The morning Sun is very beneficial to our human bodies. It is best to get morning exposures during sunrise timings.

As per the Hindu religion, praying the morning Sun God and chanting sacred 'Surya Mantra' & 'Gayatri Mantra' facing East, would be quite beneficial. Expose yourself towards the morning Sun as much as possible. Take a bath in the morning exposing to the beneficial morning Sun with better absorption of Vitamin D.

The best location for kitchen is in the South-East zone which is the fire zone. Cook facing East. The best time to cook is from 9am to 12pm.

The Sun will be at the South-East zone to benefit the Positive Ultra-Violet Rays from the Sun. After 12pm until Sunset, the immense heat of the Sun, which is not beneficial to us at all should be avoided.

After 12pm, the position of the Sun will be at South then South-West then sets at West. This is the reason why our walls at home should be thicker along the Southern and Western zone. This is to prevent the harmful UV rays of the Sun into our living premises.

ROLE OF PRANIC, JAIVIC AND SOLAR ENERGY IN VAASTU SHASTRA

In Vaastu Shastra, the traditional Indian science of architecture, the concept of energy plays a vital role in shaping the design and layout of a building or living space. Vaastu Shastra recognizes different types of energies that interact with and influence the environment. Three important types of energies in Vaastu Shastra are Pranic Energy, Jaivic Energy, and Solar Energy. Let's explore the role of each of these energies:

1. **Pranic Energy:**
    - Pranic Energy refers to the life force or vital energy that permeates all living beings and the environment.

- In Vaastu Shastra, the flow of Pranic Energy is crucial for the well-being and health of the occupants of a building.
- A well-ventilated and naturally illuminated space promotes the flow of fresh Pranic Energy, which contributes to a positive and energetic atmosphere.
- Proper ventilation allows the exchange of stagnant or negative energy with fresh, life-enhancing Pranic Energy.

2. **Jaivic Energy:**
   - Jaivic Energy is the energy present in all non-living things, such as objects, materials, and structures.
   - In Vaastu Shastra, Jaivic Energy is considered significant as it interacts with the energies of the living beings occupying the space.
   - The selection of appropriate building materials and their placement is believed to influence the Jaivic Energy and its impact on the occupants.
   - The use of natural materials like wood, stone, and clay is often preferred as they are thought to have a positive impact on the Jaivic Energy.

3. **Solar Energy:**
   - Solar Energy, as the name suggests, pertains to the influence of the Sun's energy on a building or space.
   - In Vaastu Shastra, the orientation of a building is crucial to harness the beneficial effects of Solar Energy.
   - Placing openings like doors and windows in the North and East directions allows the entry of

sunlight, which is considered beneficial for health and overall well-being.

- Solar Energy is also associated with warmth, light, and vitality, which can positively influence the occupants.

The proper balance and flow of these energies are considered essential in Vaastu Shastra to create a harmonious living or working environment. The strategic placement of rooms, doors, windows, and other architectural elements aims to maximize the positive energies and minimize the negative ones.

Vaastu Shastra practitioners often analyze these energies in combination with other factors like the five elements (Panchatatva) and the Vaastu Purush Mandala to create a space that promotes health, prosperity, and overall well-being for the occupants. It's important to note that Vaastu Shastra is a holistic science, and the consideration of these energies is just one aspect of its comprehensive approach to architecture and design

FAQ'S

a. **How do we know if a person's energy level is high or low?**

When you observe them talking negatively about people and themselves, gossiping and always complaining matters. They are never happy about themselves and the environment. Such persons are generally having very low energy level; so, they will continue to attract negative things in their lives.

b. **How do we measure a house energy level is high or low?**
Observe the North-East direction of the house. If there is an obstruction, then the house has low 'Prana' energy.

Next, observe the South-West zone. If there are no obstructions for the openings, then the 'Prana' energy has exited from this zone. The resultant effect creates a negative energy, thus making the house energy level low.

South-West zone should always be closed, heavy and with fewer openings, then the energy can be stored.

As a conclusion, leave North-East zone free and open and keep South-West zone closed and heavy and Observe the results.

As we can see, Vaastu Shastra is not a belief or a superstition. **It is a pure Science of the Cosmos**. Nothing to be 'believed' or 'worshiped'. Every principle and technique have its scientific explanation behind it; and it can be observed regardless of religion or beliefs.

3

VAASTU SHASTRA & ASTROLOGY

VAASTU SHASTRA IN-RELATION WITH ASTROLOGY – ASTRO VAASTU

Vaastu Shastra and Astrology are two ancient Indian sciences that have been practiced for thousands of years. Both of these disciplines are rooted in the belief that the cosmic energies and universal forces influence human life. While they are distinct fields, there are 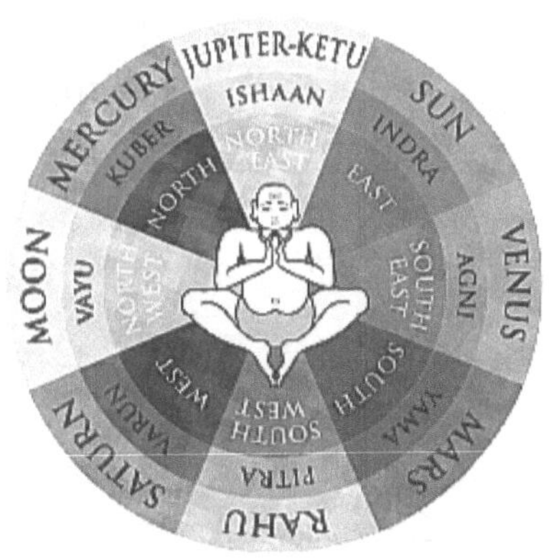

certain connections and correlations between Vaastu Shastra and Astrology. The relevance of Astrology in Vaastu Shastra can be understood through the following points:

1. **Cosmic Connection:** Both Astrology and Vaastu Shastra are based on the understanding of cosmic energies and their influence on human life. Astrology studies the positions and movements of celestial bodies like planets and stars, while Vaastu Shastra focuses on the flow of energy within the built environment. Both sciences acknowledge the interconnectedness between

the microcosm (individuals and their dwellings) and the macrocosm (the universe).

2. **Astrological Impact on Individuals:** Astrology provides insights into an individual's personality, strengths, weaknesses, and life events based on the planetary positions at the time of their birth. Vaastu Shastra takes this individuality into account when designing living spaces. It considers the astrological charts of the occupants to create customized and supportive environments that resonate with their energies. It is believed to create a positive and supportive environment that can enhance the overall well-being and success of individuals.

3. **Vaastu Purusha and Astrological Signs:** In Vaastu Shastra, the Vaastu Purusha Mandala represents the cosmic energy grid used in designing a building. The Vaastu Purusha is associated with different astrological signs, and aligning the structure with the appropriate signs is believed to attract favourable energies.

4. **Directional Alignment:** Astrology plays a role in determining the favourable directions for individuals based on their astrological charts. Vaastu Shastra considers these favourable directions when positioning various rooms, entrances, and activities within the building.

5. **Timing and Auspiciousness:** Astrology plays a role in determining auspicious timings for various activities, such as starting a new venture, conducting ceremonies, or making important decisions. Vaastu Shastra, on the other hand, helps in selecting the right direction and orientation for spaces to align with the favourable planetary energies and enhance positive outcomes.

6. **Dosha Analysis:** In both astrology and Vaastu Shastra, the concept of doshas or imbalances exists. Astrology identifies doshas in an individual's birth chart, while Vaastu Shastra identifies doshas in the design of a building. By understanding and addressing these doshas, harmonious energies can be restored.

7. **Remedial Measures:** Both Vaastu Shastra and Astrology offer remedial measures to mitigate negative influences and create a more favourable environment. For instance, in Astrology, gemstones, rituals, and prayers are prescribed to balance planetary energies, while in Vaastu Shastra, architectural adjustments, use of specific colours, and placement of certain objects are recommended to harmonize the energies in a space.

8. **Holistic Well-being:** Astrology and Vaastu Shastra share the common goal of promoting well-being and balance in an individual's life. A harmonious alignment of both sciences can provide holistic support to individuals, improving their physical, mental, and spiritual well-being.

It is essential to note that while astrology can provide valuable insights and guidance, Vaastu Shastra is a comprehensive science in itself. Combining the two sciences requires the expertise of qualified professionals who can integrate astrological principles into Vaastu design and remedies effectively. This integration ensures that the living spaces are not only aesthetically pleasing but also aligned with the cosmic energies to promote harmony and prosperity. Individuals interested in incorporating both disciplines into their lives should consult experienced professionals in each field for comprehensive guidance.

4

VAASTU SHASTRA & NUMEROLOGY

Vaastu Shastra and Numerology are interrelated with each other with respect to the directions. Every direction in Vaastu is governed by a particular planet. Each planet has its number and colour also.

Each direction has its own significance and utilization as per Vaastu Shastra.

While entering to any place may it be a house, shop, factory, prayer place, we are affected with the bio-electromagnetic radiations (energy) of that place.

This energy directly affects our soul, mind and body. If the energy is positive, we feel peaceful relaxed and our breathing slows down.

If the energy of that place is negative then immediately our breathing will increase. We feel uneasy and ultimately take wrong decisions which leads to loss of wealth, health & happiness.

To avoid all these negative aspects from life it becomes very important to follow Vaastu principles when we buy a plot, land, constructed place or construct the house, factory, office, bungalow, building etc. as it increases the chance to enjoy peaceful happy life.

RELATION BETWEEN VAASTU SHASTRA AND NUMEROLOGY

Vaastu Shastra and Numerology are both ancient Indian sciences that deal with the energy and vibrations surrounding us, but they have distinct principles and applications. However, some people believe that there is a connection between the two disciplines in terms of influencing the energies and outcomes in a person's life and living spaces. Let's explore the potential relation between Vaastu Shastra and Numerology:

1. **Energy and Vibration:** Both Vaastu Shastra and Numerology recognize the significance of energy and vibrations. Vaastu Shastra focuses on the flow of cosmic energies in the environment, while Numerology assigns vibrational qualities to numbers and names.

2. **Balancing Energies:** In Vaastu Shastra, the balance of the five elements (Panchatatva) is crucial for harmony in a space. Similarly, Numerology seeks to balance the energies associated with specific numbers to enhance a person's life.

3. **Numerology for House Numbers:** Some people use Numerology to determine the most favourable house or office number according to their birth date or other factors. They believe that a compatible number can bring positive vibrations to the space.

4. **Name Numerology:** Numerology is often employed to analyse names and determine their vibrational frequencies. In this context, people may choose to modify names or business names to align them with favourable numbers based on Numerology.

5. **Personal Numerology and Vaastu:** Some practitioners believe that a person's Numerology chart, including birth date and name, can influence the Vaastu of their living or working space. It is believed that when these energies are in harmony, it can positively impact the individual's life.

6. **Numerology for Direction Selection:** Numerology enthusiasts may use numbers associated with the individual's birth date to determine auspicious directions for specific activities or rooms within a building, aligning them with the person's favourable energies.

It's important to note that while some people find value in combining Vaastu Shastra and Numerology principles, others may follow one system independently. Both disciplines have their own methodologies and interpretations, and practitioners often have diverse viewpoints on how they can complement each other. As with any belief or practice, it's essential to approach Vaastu Shastra, Numerology, or any other system with an open mind and consider individual preferences and cultural beliefs.

RELEVANCE OF NUMEROLOGY IN VAASTU SHASTRA

Numerology and Vaastu Shastra are two distinct sciences that focus on different aspects of human life and the environment. However, some practitioners and individuals believe in integrating numerological principles with Vaastu Shastra to enhance the positive energies in living spaces. Here's the relevance of numerology in Vaastu Shastra:

1. **Personal Vibrations:** Numerology is based on the belief that each number carries a specific vibration or energy. These vibrations can influence individuals' personalities, behaviours and life events. By considering the numerological aspects of the occupants, Vaastu Shastra can create a living space that aligns with their unique energies.

2. **Numerological Analysis of Addresses:** In Vaastu Shastra, the address or plot number is considered significant. Numerology can be applied to analyse the numerological value of the address, helping in understanding its energetic influence on the occupants.

3. **Name Numerology:** Numerology is often used to analyse the numerological value of individual's names. By considering the name numerology of the occupants, Vaastu practitioners may customize the design and layout of the living space to resonate with their energies.

4. **Choosing Auspicious Dates:** Numerology can help in selecting auspicious dates for commencing construction or performing certain Vaastu-related ceremonies. An

auspicious date in numerology is believed to enhance the positive energies and success of the project.

5. **Numerological Remedies:** Numerological remedies, such as wearing specific gemstones or performing certain rituals based on an individual's numerology, can be integrated with Vaastu remedies to enhance positive energies and balance in the living space.

6. **Numerology and Vaastu Remedies:** Numerological aspects can be considered while suggesting Vaastu remedies for imbalances or doshas in a living space. The remedies may be personalized based on the numerological profiles of the occupants.

7. **Holistic Approach:** Integrating numerology with Vaastu Shastra is often seen as a holistic approach to enhancing the positive energies in living spaces. By combining the principles of both sciences, individuals may feel more connected and harmonious in their homes or workplaces.

It's important to note that while some practitioners may integrate numerology with Vaastu Shastra, these are separate sciences with different foundational principles. The relevance of numerology in Vaastu Shastra depends on individual beliefs and preferences. For those interested in combining the two sciences, it is recommended to consult experienced professionals who have expertise in both numerology and Vaastu Shastra to ensure a balanced and effective integration.

THE CALCULATION AND TABLE FORM – CORELATING NUMEROLOGY & VAASTU SHASTRA

With this technique of knowing the lucky and destiny number of our self, we can find the right direction for us.

Most of us know own date of birth. Suppose your birth day is on 11th then add the date to single digit. It comes to 1+1=2. Now add the total date of birth.

If it is 11th May 1978 than add all the numbers to single digit that is 1+1+0+5+1+9+7+8=32=3+2=5.

This way by adding the day and full date of birth we got two numbers, 2 as Lucky number and 5 as Destiny number.

Now, let us co-relate our Lucky number and Destiny number with the Eight Directions and its ruling number with the help of below table.

A TABLE DEPICTING VAASTU SHASTRA IN-RELATION WITH NUMEROLOGY

Direction	Planet	Ruling Number
East	Sun	1 (One)
North	Mercury	5 (Five)
South	Mars	9 (Nine)
West	Saturn	8 (Eight)
North-East	Jupiter / Ketu	3 / 7 (Three / Seven)
South-East	Venus	6 (Six)
North-West	Moon	2 (Two)
South-West	Rahu	4 (Four)

While Vaastu shastra gives us information about our lucky directions that can aid in positive energy, Numerology gives us the numbers behind those directions which obviously bring more luck and prosperity to the residents of any particular household.

5

VAASTU SHASTRA & COLOUR THERAPY

RELATION BETWEEN VAASTU SHASTRA AND COLOUR THERAPY – CHROMOTHERAPY

Vaastu Shastra and **Chromotherapy** (also known as colour therapy) are two distinct systems with different approaches but share a common belief in the influence of colours on human emotions, energies, and well-being. Let's explore the potential relationship between Vaastu Shastra and Chromotherapy:

1. **Colours in Vaastu Shastra:** Vaastu Shastra emphasizes the significance of colours in creating a balanced and harmonious living or working environment. Different colours are associated with specific elements and directions, and they are believed to influence the flow of energy (prana) in a space.

2. **Colours and the Five Elements:** In Vaastu Shastra, each colour is associated with one of the five elements (Panchatatva) – Earth (Prithvi), Water (Ap/Jal), Fire (Tejas), Air (Vayu), and Space (Akasha). Using appropriate colours in specific areas of a building is believed to balance the elements and enhance the overall harmony.

3. **Colour for Direction and Purpose:** Vaastu Shastra suggests using specific colours for different directions and rooms. For example, light blue or green is often recommended for the East direction, which represents new beginnings and growth.

4. **Chromotherapy and Healing:** Chromotherapy, on the other hand, is a holistic healing practice that uses colours to influence physical, emotional, and mental well-being. Each colour is associated with certain healing properties and can be used to balance the body's energy centres (chakras).

5. **Colour Psychology:** Both Vaastu Shastra and Chromotherapy recognize the psychological impact of colours on human emotions and moods. Colours can evoke specific feelings and reactions, and their use in the environment can affect a person's overall experience.

6. **Integration of Colours:** Some practitioners and interior designers incorporate both Vaastu Shastra principles and Chromotherapy when designing living or working spaces. They may choose colours based on Vaastu guidelines for specific directions while also considering the therapeutic effects of colours on occupants.

It's important to note that while there may be a connection in the belief of colours influence on energies and well-being, Vaastu Shastra and Chromotherapy are separate disciplines with their own unique principles and practices. Some people may choose to apply both systems together, while others may prefer one over the other based on their personal beliefs and preferences.

As with any holistic approach, it's essential to approach Vaastu Shastra and Chromotherapy with an open mind and consider individual needs and cultural beliefs. If you are interested in incorporating colours based on Vaastu principles or Chromotherapy into your living or working space, you may seek guidance from qualified practitioners or experts in these respective fields.

COLOURS AND THEIR MEANING AS PER VAASTU

Colours play a vital role in influencing our behaviour, our thought processes and also in creating specific atmospheres in the house. Vaastu colours help one target and maximize certain kinds of energy in different spaces in the house such as bedroom, meditation room, living room etc.

Every colour has specific properties and characteristics and an understanding of these colours is essential for a harmonious and prosperous living.

Yellow signifies wisdom and patience. This colour is great for rooms which do not get direct sunlight. Apart from this, yellow is also auspicious for puja rooms and study rooms.

Orange symbolizes power and spirituality. This colour symbolises happiness, optimism and healthy relationships. Subtle shades of orange are some of the best Vaastu-colours for homes and can be used anywhere.

Blue is the colour of sky as well as water. Blue signifies new beginnings, emotions, inspiration, devotion and truth. This shade is excellent for bedrooms and meditation rooms.

Red signifies power and bravery. However, avoid using red in bedrooms as it has an aggressive quality attached to it; which may get overwhelming and affect personal relationships.

Purple inspires trust. Lighter shades of purple can be used for a calm and soothing environment.

Beige is a colour of happiness, peace and purity. It can be applied to the walls in the west direction and is also a good colour for the library.

Green symbolizes hope. It offers healing, harmonious and a positive atmosphere. It is an auspicious colour for study rooms.

White is a graceful and pure colour, which looks good when blended with other hues. It is always advisable to have white ceilings.

IMPACT OF VAASTU COLOURS AND ITS RELEVANCE IN A RESIDENTIAL HOUSE

Vaastu Shastra, an ancient Indian architectural and design system, places significant importance on colours in residential homes. According to Vaastu principles, colours are believed to influence the energy and vibrations within a space, which can impact the well-being, harmony, and prosperity of the occupants. Here's an overview of the impact of Vaastu colours and their relevance in a residential house:

1. **Psychological and Emotional Impact:**
    *   **Warm Colours (Red, Orange, Yellow):** These colours are associated with warmth, energy, and positivity. They can promote enthusiasm, creativity, and a sense of well-being when used appropriately.
    *   **Cool Colours (Blue, Green, Purple):** Cool colours are calming and soothing. They can help create a peaceful and tranquil environment, making them suitable for bedrooms and meditation spaces.
    *   **Neutral Colours (White, Beige, Gray):** Neutral colours are versatile and can be used to create a sense of balance and neutrality. White, in particular, is often used to symbolize purity and clarity.

2. **Spatial Perception and Size:**
    Light colours can make a room appear more spacious, while dark colours can make it feel cozier and smaller. Proper use of colours can help balance the perception of space and improve the flow of energy within rooms.

3. **Balance of Elements:**
    Vaastu emphasizes the balance of the five elements (Panchatatva) in a space: earth, water, fire, air, and space. Different colours are associated with these elements, and using them appropriately can create a harmonious environment. For example, earthy colours like brown and yellow represent the earth element, while blue and green represent the water element.

4. **Directional Significance:**
    Vaastu assigns specific colours to different directions of a home. For instance, the north direction is associated

with water, so cool and watery colours like blue or green are recommended for rooms in the northern part of the house. South is associated with fire, so warm colours like red or orange may be suitable for the southern areas.

5. **Personal Preferences and Culture:**
   Personal preferences and cultural influences play a role in colour choices. While Vaastu provides guidelines, it's important to consider what colours resonate with the occupants and align with their cultural and aesthetic preferences.

6. **Correcting Vaastu Imbalances:**
   In some cases, specific colours are recommended to correct Vaastu imbalances in a house. For example, if a certain area has negative energy, using colours associated with the element related to that direction can help mitigate the imbalance.

It's important to note that while Vaastu offers colour guidelines, it is also flexible and adaptable to individual circumstances. The key is to create a harmonious and balanced living environment. If you're interested in applying Vaastu principles to your home, you should consult with a Vaastu expert who can provide personalized recommendations based on your specific space and needs. Additionally, personal well-being and preferences should always be taken into consideration when choosing colours for your home.

6

VAASTU TIPS – RESIDENTIAL, OFFICIAL, COMMERCIAL & INDUSTRIAL SPACES

A) HOUSE VAASTU

VAASTU TIPS FOR A RESIDENTIAL BUILDING

Vaastu Shastra, the ancient Indian science of architecture, provides guidelines for creating a harmonious and positive living environment in a residential building. By following these Vaastu tips, you can enhance the flow of positive energy (prana) and create a conducive space for overall well-being and prosperity. Here are some Vaastu tips for a residential building:

1. **Main Entrance:**
   - The main entrance should face a positive direction, preferably North, East, or Northeast, to allow the inflow of positive energy.
   - The entrance should be well-lit, inviting, and free from obstacles or clutter.
2. **Living Room:**
   - Place the living room in the North or East direction for a vibrant and energetic atmosphere.

- Use bright and cheerful colors to create a welcoming space for social interactions.

3. **Bedroom Placement:**
   - Position the master bedroom in the Southwest direction for better rest and stability.
   - Avoid placing the bed under overhead beams, as it may create stress and discomfort.

4. **Kitchen Location:**
   - Place the kitchen in the Southeast corner of the house. This direction is associated with the fire element and supports better health and nourishment.
   - Ensure proper ventilation in the kitchen to keep the energy fresh.

5. **Bathroom and Toilet:**
   - Locate the bathrooms and toilets in the Northwest or West direction.
   - Keep the bathrooms clean and well-maintained to avoid negative energy.

6. **Children's Room:**
   - If possible, place the children's room in the West or Northwest direction.
   - Use calming colors and decor to promote a positive and creative atmosphere.

7. **Study or Home Office:**
   - Position the study or home office in the North or East direction for enhanced focus and productivity.
   - Ensure ample natural light and a clutter-free environment.

8. **Ventilation and Natural Light:**
   - Ensure proper ventilation in all rooms to allow fresh air circulation.
   - Maximize natural light by using large windows and keeping the space uncluttered.

9. **Indoor Plants:**
   Place indoor plants in the living area and other rooms to purify the air and add a touch of nature.

10. **Water Elements:**
    - A small water fountain or aquarium in the North or East direction can enhance positive energy flow.
    - Avoid placing water elements in the bedroom or the South direction.

11. **Storage and Clutter Management:**
    - Keep the living space tidy and clutter-free. Clutter can obstruct the flow of positive energy.
    - Regularly declutter and organize your belongings.

12. **Electromagnetic Fields (EMFs):**
    Minimize the use of electronic devices in the bedroom, especially near the bed, to promote better sleep.

13. **Outdoor Space:**
    Create a pleasant outdoor space, such as a garden or patio, in the North or East direction for relaxation and rejuvenation.

14. **Intention and Mindfulness:**
    Your intention and mindfulness play a crucial role in creating a positive environment. Infuse your home with positive thoughts, prayers, and good intentions.

Remember that Vaastu tips for a residential building are meant to be applied in conjunction with other healthy lifestyle practices. It's essential to customize these tips based on your specific living space, needs, and cultural considerations. For personalized advice, consider consulting with a qualified Vaastu expert who can offer specific recommendations for your residential building.

Visual Representation of the Location and Orientation of all possible House areas depicted in a Grid format as per Vaastu Principles.

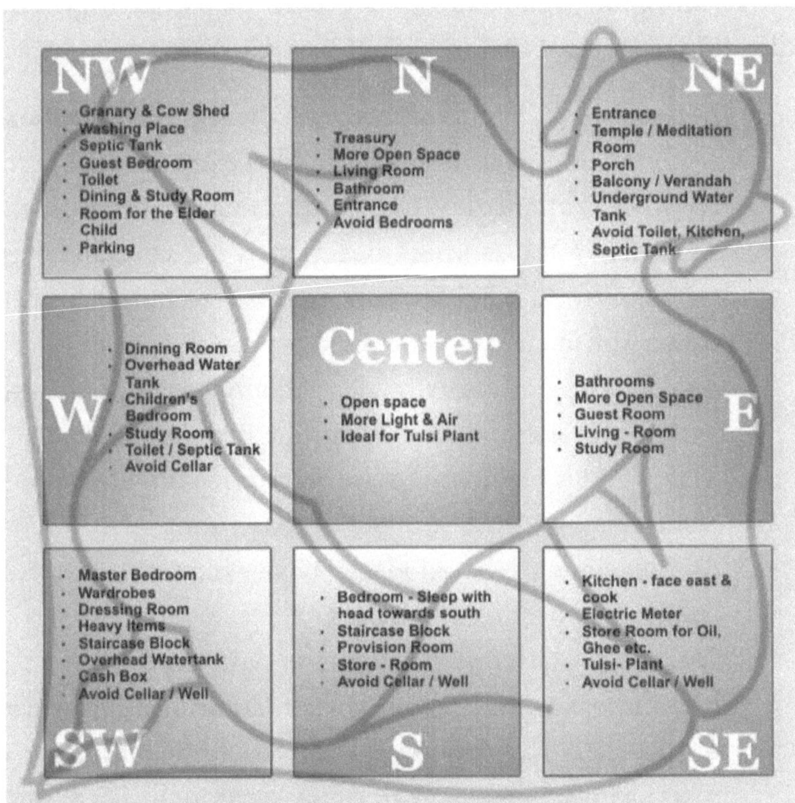

VASTU TIPS FOR DOORS & WINDOWS

According to Vaastu Shastra doors and windows can make a huge difference to peace, prosperity, and luck of a house hold.

Doors and windows are not merely passages for people to enter, but are also for positive and negative energies to enter in the house.

If a window is made in the wrong direction, it is a gateway for the negative energies to come in and can harm the inhabitants.

If the doors and windows are constructed in the right direction, they can bring in a lot of prosperity and good luck.

1. A doorway constructed towards the eastern direction is considered very auspicious. However, we can also construct entrances in the western and northern sides. An entry in the southern direction is not considered as suitable. Avoid making doors or windows in south-west corners of the house, office or any property.
2. Avoid having any sort of obstructions, such as plants, temple and staircases in front of the main entrance.
3. Teak wood is considered to be best for making doors and windows.
4. All the windows should ideally be of symmetrical shapes and be proportionate in height.
5. Doors must never be placed at the centre of a wall.
6. It is important to keep cross-ventilation in mind while fitting doors and windows. They should be placed such that maximum light and air can pass through. Therefore,

it is suggested that doors and windows be placed opposite each other.

7. According to Vaastu for house structure, a house must at all times have even numbers of windows and door (e.g., 2, 4, 6, 8, etc.).

1) ENTRANCE :-
BEST POSITIONS - NE / N / E / S of SE / W of NW

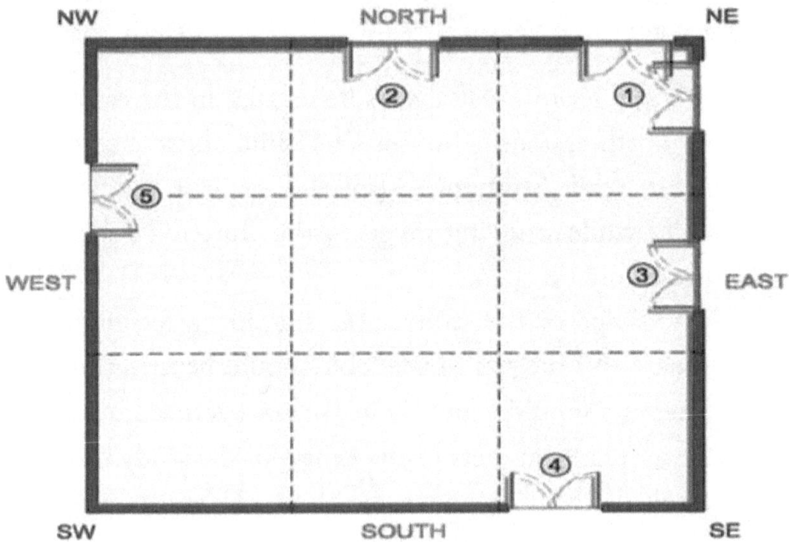

Preferable location of Main doors marked as per Vaastu Grid

VASTU TIPS FOR PLACEMENT OF STUDY ROOM

Study rooms built according to Vaastu Shastra helps in enhancing the grasping and concentration powers of children, thereby giving them a boost to do well academically.

Vaastu tips also help in reducing the exam stress thereby facilitating academic success.

Here are some Vaastu tips and advice for a study room.

1. A study room must always be located in the east, north or north-east of a house. The child must face east or north while studying. Also, the space in front of the child while studying must not be cluttered and should preferably be open.
2. The shape of the study table should be rectangular or square and the size of the table should be medium.
3. Students should avoid sitting below overhead beams.
4. Never place cabinets in the centre of the study room.
5. Book shelves must never be above the study table. The study table should not be cluttered by books.
6. Table lamps enhances a child's concentration. The study room should be well lit.
7. Bright colours such as yellow, pink and orange in the study room improves the child's concentration.

B) OFFICE VAASTU

VAASTU APPLICATIONS FOR AN OFFICE BUILDING

Applying Vaastu principles to an office building can help to create a positive and harmonious working environment, which may contribute to the productivity and well-being of employees. Here are some Vaastu applications for an office building:

1. **Site Selection:** Choose a plot or location for the office building that is free from obstructions and has a regular or square shape. The plot should ideally be situated in an area with a balanced energy flow.

2. **Main Entrance:** Position the main entrance of the office building in a favourable direction, such as North, East, or Northeast, to attract positive energy. Keep the entrance well-lit, spacious, and free from obstacles.

3. **Reception Area:** The reception area should be well-organized and located near the entrance. It should be aesthetically pleasing and create a positive first impression for visitors.

4. **Office Layout:** Design the office layout in a way that maximizes natural light and ventilation. Keep the workspace open and clutter-free to allow the smooth flow of energy.

5. **Directional Placement:** Arrange different departments or sections of the office based on their association with specific directions. For example, place the administrative

offices in the South or West direction, and the sales or marketing team in the North or Northwest direction.

6. **Cabin Placement:** Position the cabins of senior management or executives in the South, Southwest, or West direction. This can provide them with a sense of stability and authority.

7. **Employee Seating:** Ensure that employees workstations face the East or North direction, as this is believed to enhance concentration and productivity.

8. **Conference Rooms:** Place conference rooms in the North or East direction. These directions are associated with good communication and decision-making.

9. **Pantry and Kitchen:** Locate the pantry or kitchen in the Southeast direction, which is associated with the fire element and supports better nourishment and energy.

10. **Toilets and Restrooms:** Position toilets and restrooms in the Northwest or West direction. Keep them clean and well-maintained to avoid negative energy.

11. **Colour Scheme:** Use a colour scheme that promotes a professional and positive ambiance. Colours like white, light blue, and green are generally considered auspicious for office spaces.

12. **Indoor Plants:** Place indoor plants strategically to purify the air and add a touch of nature. Avoid using thorny or dried plants.

13. **Electromagnetic Fields (EMFs):** Minimize the use of electronic devices and electrical equipment in workspaces to reduce EMF exposure.

14. **Furniture and Fixtures:** Position furniture and fixtures in a way that allows for easy movement and functionality. Avoid sharp edges or corners.

15. **Outdoor Space:** If possible, create a pleasant outdoor space for employees to take breaks and rejuvenate. A well-maintained garden or seating area can enhance the office environment.

Remember that Vaastu principles for an office building can be adapted based on the specific size, layout, and requirements of the space. It's essential to consider practicality and functionality while incorporating Vaastu guidelines into the office design. Additionally, consulting with a qualified Vaastu expert can provide more personalized recommendations based on the specific needs and goals of the office building.

Vaastu Shastra tips to create a conducive and positive working environment – to get the work done more efficiently and effectively.

Vaastu for offices, considers many factors like proper location of the office, office exteriors in terms of its slope, shape etc, direction in which different departments of the office and the reception are located, position of various electronic gadgets and many more.

1. Northern and Eastern zones will be good for seating for the middle managers

2. North-West portion for the field staff

3. Accounts department should be in the South-East direction

4. Cabins for Senior/top management preferably in South-west direction.

5. Reception counter is North-East portion of the office

6. It is always advisable to have a rectangular work-stations.

7. The functional location for the pantry/electrical & electronic gadgets is South-East direction.

Visual Representation of the Location and Orientation of all possible Office areas depicted in a Grid format as per Vaastu Principles.

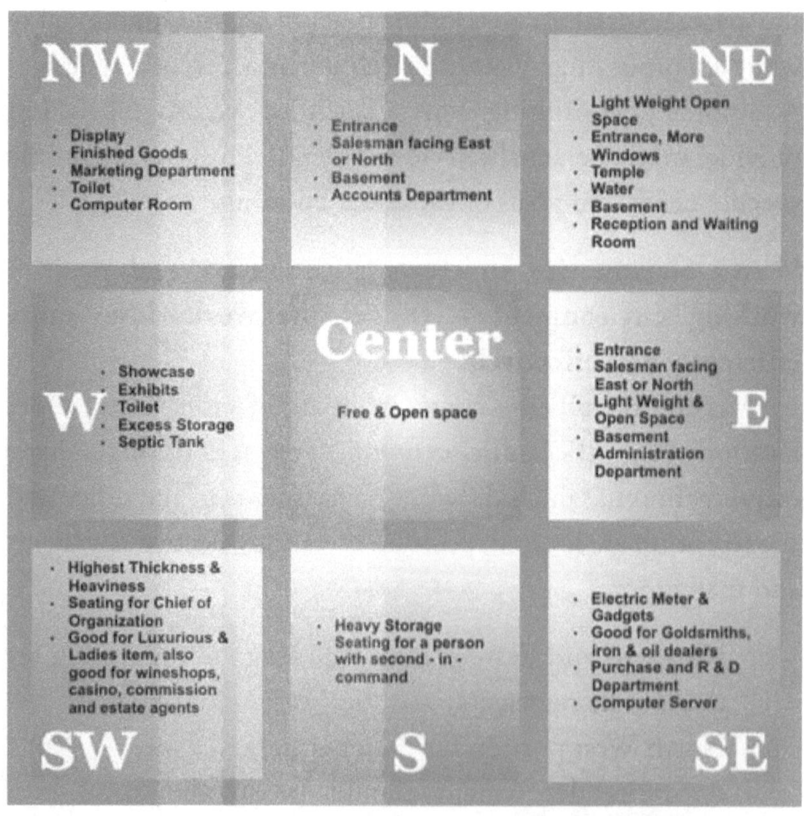

C) SHOP VAASTU

VAASTU TIPS FOR A SHOP ESTABLISHMENT

Applying Vaastu principles while establishing a shop can create a positive and inviting environment that may attract customers and promote business success. Here are some Vaastu tips for a shop establishment:

1. **Location and Entrance:**
   - Choose a location for the shop that receives good footfall and visibility. The shop entrance should be prominent and well-lit.
   - Preferably, the entrance should face a positive direction, such as North, East, or Northeast, to attract positive energy and customers.

2. **Shop Layout:**
   - Design the shop layout with an open and clutter-free space to allow the smooth flow of customers.
   - Avoid irregular shapes and protrusions in the shop, as they can create imbalances in energy.

3. **Cash Counter:**
   Place the cash counter in the Southeast direction of the shop. This is associated with the element of fire and is believed to promote financial stability.

4. **Product Display:**
   - Arrange the products neatly and systematically on shelves. Keep the display area well-lit and attractive to catch the attention of customers.
   - Consider placing popular or high-margin items in the front area to attract customers.

5. **Colour Scheme:**
   - Use bright and vibrant colours in the shop to create a positive and energetic ambiance.
   - Colours like yellow, orange, and green are generally considered auspicious for commercial spaces.

6. **Signage:**
   Ensure that the shop's name or signage is clear, visible, and well-illuminated, especially near the entrance.

7. **Furniture and Fixtures:**
   - Position the furniture, such as racks and counters, in a way that allows a smooth and easy flow of customers.
   - Avoid sharp corners and edges in the furniture, as they may create discomfort for customers.

8. **Natural Light and Ventilation:**
   - Maximize natural light and ventilation in the shop to maintain a fresh and positive atmosphere.
   - Use large windows and keep the space clutter-free to facilitate good airflow.

9. **Indoor Plants:**
   - Place indoor plants strategically in the shop to purify the air and add a touch of nature.
   - Avoid using thorny or dried plants inside the shop.

10. **Music and Sound:**
    Play soft and soothing background music to create a pleasant shopping experience for customers.

11. **Electromagnetic Fields (EMFs):**
    Minimize the use of electronic devices, especially near the cash counter and customer seating areas.

12. **Cleanliness and Maintenance:**
    Keep the shop clean, well-maintained, and free from clutter to attract positive energy and customers.

It's important to customize these Vaastu tips based on the specific size, layout, and requirements of your shop. If possible, consult with a qualified Vaastu expert who can provide personalized advice and suggestions tailored to your shop's unique situation. Remember that while Vaastu tips can create a positive environment, other factors such as product quality, customer service, and marketing efforts are also essential for the success of your shop.

Visual Representation of the Location and Orientation of all possible Shop areas depicted in a Grid format as per Vaastu Principles.

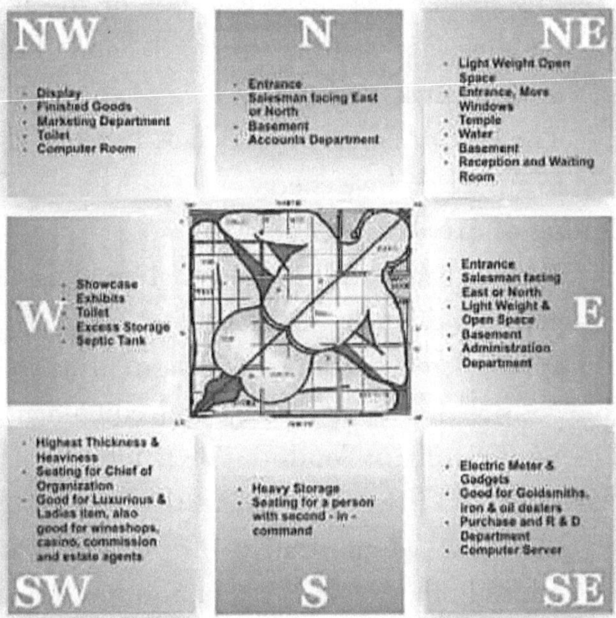

D) INDUSTRY / FACTORY VAASTU

Applying Vaastu principles in an industrial building can help to create a balanced and harmonious working environment, which may positively impact productivity and overall well-being. Here are some Vaastu guidelines for an industrial building:

1. **Plot Selection:**
   - Choose a plot with regular or square shape for the industrial building. Avoid plots with irregular shapes or cuts.
   - If possible, select a plot with the main entrance facing North, East, or Northeast for positive energy flow.

2. **Main Entrance:**
   - Ensure that the main entrance of the industrial building is well-lit, spacious, and free from obstructions.
   - The entrance should ideally face a positive direction to attract positive energy.

3. **Zoning of Areas:**
   - Plan the layout of the industrial building carefully, placing different sections or departments in appropriate zones based on Vaastu principles.
   - Position heavy machinery and equipment in the West, South, or Southwest direction.

4. **Placement of Offices and Cabins:**
   - Place the administrative offices and managerial cabins in the South, West, or Southwest direction.

- Ensure that the seating arrangement in offices and cabins allows the occupant to face either North or East while working.

5. **Factory Floor and Manufacturing Area:**
   - The factory floor and manufacturing area should ideally be in the East, North, or Northeast direction.
   - Keep this area clean, organized, and well-lit to enhance productivity.

6. **Storage and Warehouse:**
   - The storage or warehouse area should be in the West or Southwest direction.
   - Keep this area clutter-free and organized for smooth movement of goods.

7. **Toilets and Restrooms:**
   - Position the toilets and restrooms in the Northwest or West direction of the building.
   - Keep these areas clean and well-ventilated.

8. **Ventilation and Natural Light:**
   - Ensure proper ventilation in all areas of the industrial building to maintain a fresh and healthy working environment.
   - Maximize the use of natural light by incorporating large windows and skylights.

9. **Avoid Obstructions:**
   - Avoid irregularities, extensions, or protrusions in the Northeast direction, as this may hinder the flow of positive energy.

10. **Utilities and Services:**
    - Place utility rooms and services such as generators, electrical panels, and water pumps in the Southeast direction.
11. **Electromagnetic Fields (EMFs):**
    - Minimize the use of electronic devices and electrical equipment in office and rest areas.
12. **Outdoor Space:**
    - Create a well-maintained outdoor space, such as a garden or open area, on the North or East side of the building for employees to relax during breaks.
13. **Colour Scheme:**
    - Use colours that promote a professional and positive ambiance in management offices and common areas.

It's essential to remember that Vaastu principles for an industrial building may need to be adapted based on the specific requirements and limitations of the industry and the building design.

Consulting with a qualified Vaastu expert who has experience in industrial spaces can help to tailor the Vaastu tips to suit your unique situation and optimize the working environment for productivity and prosperity.

VAASTU TIPS FOR INDUSTRY / FACTORY

Application of Vaastu principles for industry ensures the successful production and profitable business.

a. The building construction of the industry or factory should be in the South-West portion of the plot

b. More of open space should be kept on the Northern and Eastern sides

c. The right place for the installation Water Tank is North-East

d. The ideal place for storing the raw material lies in the Western portion

e. The finished goods should be packed and placed on the North-West side

f. The ideal location for constructing administrative area is Northern or Eastern side

g. For staff quarters, the right place is in South-East or North-West zone

h. Lawn and Landscaping should be done in the North or East

Visual Representation of the Location and Orientation of all possible Industrial / Factory areas depicted in a Grid format as per Vaastu Principles.

	North West	North	North East	
	✓ Side Entrance ✓ Finished Products ✓ Toilets ✓ Guardroom ✓ Staff Quarters ✓ Parking For Trucks Etc.,	✓ Main Entrance ✓ Office-Owner Should Face North ✓ Septic Tank ✓ Finished Products	✓ Main entrance ✓ Parking for cycles, scooters etc., ✓ Borewells, underground tanks, oil store etc., ✓ Meditation place ✓ Finished products ✗ Avoid overhead tanks	
West	✓ Compound should never be vacant-storage for raw materials ✓ Storage for heavy machinery		✓ Main Entrance ✓ Office owner face East ✓ CAO block ✓ More open space	**East**
	✓ Heavy Machinery Store ✓ Raw Materials ✓ Office of MD or Owner ✗ Avoid Septic Tank	✓ Never keep vacant ✓ Store for heavy machinery, raw materials etc.,	✓ Transformers, boilers, generators etc., ✓ Toilet ✓ Guard Room	
	South West	South	South East	

7

VAASTUTATVAH & ITS VARIOUS ASPECTS w.r.t '8' DIRECTIONS & 'BRAHMASTHAN' – (TF)

SR.	DESCRIPTION	1 NORTH	2 NORTH-EAST	3 EAST	4 SOUTH-EAST
1	**DIVINE LOCATION**	Shoulder of the vastu purush	Head of the vastu purush	Shoulder of the vastu purush	Arm and Thigh of the vastu purush
2	**RULING GOD**	Kubera	Ishaanya	Indra (King of God)	Agni (God of Fire)
3	**RULING PLANET**	Budha (Mercury)	Guru (Jupiter)	Surya (Sun)	Shukra (Venus)
4	**ELEMENTS**	Water (Jal Tatva)	Water (Jal)	Light, power	Fire (Agni)
5	**EMBODIMENT**	Wealth and career	Knowledge and spiritual wealth	Fertility, wealth, children	Health, women's issues
6	**RECOMMENDED SPACES**	Treasury and main entrance	This is a space for worship, meditation, wells, underground tanks, boring wells,study room.	Dinning hall, more doors and windows on east side, childrens bedroom, study room	Kitchen, fireplace, electrical equipments, entertainment room

5	6	7	8	9
SOUTH	**SOUTH-WEST**	**WEST**	**NORTH-WEST**	**CENTRE-BRAHMASTHAN**
Ankle of the vastu purush	Feet of the vastu	Ankle of the vastu purush	Arm & Thigh of vastu purush	Naval of vastu purush
Yama (God of Dharma & Death)	Nirtti (Lord of Demons)	Varun (God of Water & Rain)	Vaayu (God of Wind)	Brahma (Creator)
Mangal (Mars)	Rahu	Shani (Saturn)	Moon	Ravi (Sun)
Earth	Earth	Air, moisture	Air	Space
Life and death, legal affairs and struggle	Fame, income, longevity	Fate, karma, fame, wealth	Communication, social Life, business, travel	Balance & creativity, spiritual growth
Bedrooms, stores, grain store	Master bedroom, store rooms, very important rooms	Services, toilets, bedrooms, study-room	Accounts area, guest room, servents room,	Sitting room, drawing room, prescribed to keep the area vacant as vastu purush breathes through these open spaces

SR.	DESCRIPTION	1 NORTH	2 NORTH-EAST	3 EAST	4 SOUTH-EAST
7	**AVOID**	Toilet and fire places	Heavy objects and structures, master – bedrooms, toilets, Kitchen.	Toilet.	Water bodies and open varendah
8	**COLOUR**	Light blue, pale colours, light green, off white, beige, white	Bright yellow, bright white	Orange, yellow, shining white	Warm colors, sky blue, silver white
9	**SHAPES**	Rectangles and polylines	Regular linear shape, squares	Star, hexagon	Half moon shape, elliptical
10	**PLANT**	Palm, pakad, neem, bilva, shami, kaith, tulsi	Basil, herbs , aamla	Lavender, rose, bergamot, bamboo, bargad	Herbs, mint, basil, roses, annar

5	6	7	8	9
SOUTH	**SOUTH-WEST**	**WEST**	**NORTH-WEST**	**CENTRE-BRAHMASTHAN**
Living rooms, underground water tank, pits, septic tanks	Pits, wells, septic tanks, water storage tanks, open balcony	Septic tank, wells, pits	Tall structure and trees should not be built in this direction.	Heavily built structures, staircase, kitchen and toilet
All earth color, brown, red, pink, blue	All earth colors, purple, grey, blue, green	Beige, peach, dull – white, light green	Light blue, dull white, pista green, white	White, bright yellow
Irregular shapes and triangles	Square, cubes, stable forms	Circular, elliptical	Square, rectangle	All solid shapes, squares
Rose, neem, cotton, udumbara (Goolar) & panas etc are favorable towards south	Heavy leaf bearing trees like ashoka, neem, banyan, emli, are best suited in the southwest zone	Bilva, kair, neelgiri, madhuka and peepal are very favourable on the west of the house limit	Bail patra /wood apple, cactu	Tulsi (basil)

CHOGHADIYA

1. **CHOGHADIYA – INTRODUCTION & ITS CALCULATION**
2. **CHOGHADIYA & ITS RELATION TO ASTROLOGY**
3. **IDENTIFYING MEANING OF DIFFERENT CHOGHADIYA IN A TABLE**
4. **DAY & NIGHT CHOGHADIYA – (TF)**

1

CHOGHADIYA – INTRODUCTION & ITS CALCULATION

Choghadiya Muhurat a part of the Vedic Hindu calendar, **'Panchang'**. It is an ancient measure for calculating time in India and popular in North India, roughly equivalent to 24 minutes in each division. The origin of Choghadiya can be traced back to the Vedic period in India. It is believed that this system was first mentioned in 'Rigveda', one of Hinduism's oldest sacred texts.

An astrologer is consulted to obtain (calculate) a good Muhurat – (an auspicious period for the fulfilment of a particular task performed at that period of time) to be fruitful.

People believe in performing life-related important task according to a suitable Muhurat in India.

We believe with an immense importance to that particular Muhurat and perform the task we desire to pursue as per that Muhurat.

MEANING, RELEVANCE AND APPLICATION OF CHOGHADIYA IN HINDUISM

Choghadiya is a concept in Hindu astrology and Vedic shastra that is used to determine auspicious and inauspicious times for various activities. It plays a significant role in Hinduism and is particularly relevant for selecting auspicious timings for important events and rituals. Here's a closer look at the meaning, relevance, and application of Choghadiya in Hinduism:

1. **Meaning of Choghadiya:**
    *   The term "Choghadiya" is derived from two words: "Choghadi" (four parts) and "Ya" (unit of time). It refers to dividing the day and night into eight time periods, each of approximately 1.5 hours.

2. **Relevance in Hinduism:**
    *   Choghadiya is deeply rooted in Hinduism and is considered a crucial tool for determining the most favourable times to initiate important activities, ceremonies, or journeys.
    *   It is often used to avoid inauspicious times, known as "Rog" or "Kaalam," when unfavourable planetary influences are believed to be stronger.

3. **Application in Hindu Rituals and Events:**
    *   Choghadiya is widely applied in various Hindu rituals and events, including but not limited to:
    *   **Weddings:** Selecting an auspicious Choghadiya is a common practice during Hindu weddings to ensure a harmonious and prosperous marital life.
    *   **Business and Investments:** Entrepreneurs and traders often use Choghadiya to commence new business ventures or make significant investments.
    *   **Travel:** Choosing an auspicious Choghadiya is believed to ensure a safe and successful journey.
    *   **Religious Ceremonies:** Choghadiya is consulted when performing religious ceremonies, such as

havans, pujas, and yagnas, to ensure the desired spiritual outcomes.

- **Naming of Children:** Some parents use Choghadiya to choose an auspicious time for naming their newborn child.

4. **Calculation of Choghadiya:**
   - Choghadiya is calculated based on the position of the planets and their influence on different parts of the day and night.
   - The eight time periods are categorized into four groups: Shubh (auspicious), Laabh (profitable), Amrut (nectar), and Chal (inauspicious). Each group has two time periods.
   - The calculation of Choghadiya requires knowledge of astrology and is often done by astrologers or specialized software.

5. **Variations and Regional Differences:**
   - Different regions in India may have variations in Choghadiya calculations and names.
   - Some practitioners may also consider the specific planetary hours, known as "Hora," when selecting auspicious times.

6. **Spiritual Significance:**
   - Choghadiya is viewed as a means of aligning one's activities with the cosmic energies and favourable planetary influences, which are believed to enhance the chances of success and positive outcomes.

It's important to note that while Choghadiya holds deep cultural and spiritual significance in Hinduism, its effectiveness and relevance are a matter of belief and faith. Some people strictly adhere to Choghadiya for important decisions, while others may consider it as a guideline or cultural tradition. The application of Choghadiya is a personal choice, and individuals may choose to use it based on their beliefs and cultural practices.

LITERARY MEANING OF CHOGHADIYA & ITS CALCULATION AS PER VEDIC SHASTRA IN HINDUISM

Choghadiya is = **'Cho'** + **'Ghadi'**. The word "Cho" means four and in Vedic Astrology, time is measured in Ghadi.

1 Ghadi is equal to 24 minutes. So Choghadiya means the period of four Ghadi which is equal to 96 minutes or 1 and 1/2 half hours approximately.

METHOD OF CALCULATION

The time from Sunrise to Sunset is divided into 8 equal parts to calculate day time, popularly known as Din Ka Choghadiya.

Time from Sunset until the next day Sunrise is divided into another 8 equal parts to calculate night time, known as Raat Ka Choghadiya.

There is a total of 16 Choghadiya Muhurats in 24 hours and each is categorized into Good or Bad Muhurat.

All of these parts are equal but the duration of each part greatly depends on the location of that particular place, as the days and nights are longer and shorter at different places at different period of time.

GENERAL INTERPRETATION:

Each day is divided into two time periods:

Daytime – the period from sunrise to sunset and Night time – the period from sunset to sunrise.

Each period contains eight Choghadiya's. The daytime difference is arrived at by calculating the difference between Sunrise and Sunset and dividing the same by 8.

Example:

Day 1: **Sunrise at 6:00 AM and Sunset at 6:01 pm** & Day 2: **Sunrise at 6:00 am based on the above.** The daytime period is 12 hours and 01 minutes (721 minutes). The night time period is 11 hours and 59 minutes (719 minutes).

Therefore, each daytime Choghadiya lasts 721/8 = 90.125 minutes = 1 hour 30 minutes 7.5 seconds and each night-time Choghadiya last 719/8 = 89.87 minutes = 1 hour 29 minutes 52.5 second.

ASTROLOGICAL INTERPRETATION OF CHOGHADIYA

To calculate Choghadiya Muhurat, daytime and nightime are divided into eight equal parts and each time division is known as Choghadiya. As each division approximately equals to four Ghadi, this division of time is known as Choghadiya or **Chaturshtika Muhurat**

Any Choghadiya division could be good or bad depending on the weekday and time of the day

The first Choghadiya of the day is decided based on the ruling deity of that day.

So, on Sunday the first Choghadiya Muhurat is ruled by the Sun followed by Venus, Mercury, Moon, Saturn, Jupiter and Sun.

The prevailing Lord during the Choghadiya division makes it bad or good.

While selecting Choghadiya Muhurat adverse time of Vaar Vela, Kaal Vela and Kaal Ratri – (Time with Malefic effect) should be rejected as these might overlap with auspicious Muhurat timings.

It is believed that all auspicious activities performed during Vaar Vela, Kaal Vela and Kaal Ratri are not fruitful.

A) SHUBH CHOGHADIYA MUHURATS

Four Shubh Choghadiya is mentioned in all authentic Muhurat Principles. They are **Amrit, Shubh, Labh, and Char.**

Amrit Choghadiya means free from bad influence, long lasting and it is the best time to pray to God.

Shubh means good, blessed and Griha Pravesh should be done in this period.

Labh means gains and usually business started in this period shows huge gains.

Sometimes, Good Choghadiya is neutralized by bad muhurat like Rahu Kaal (Time with Malefic effects)

B) BAD CHOGHADIYA MUHURATS

Bad Choghadiya names are **Kaal Vela, Vaar Vela, Udveg and Kaal Ratri.**

Auspicious work should be avoided during Vaar Vela, Kaal Vela, Udveg as mentioned by all Muhurat Principles.

Kaal Ratri is malefic of all and must be avoided.

Kaal Vela and Vaar Vela come in the daytime while Kaal Ratri comes during night time.

If Good Choghadiya is overlapping with Bad Choghadiya then that Muhurat should be avoided.

2

CHOUGHADIYA & ITS RELATION TO ASTROLOGY

The Vedic Hindu calendar interprets Choghadiya as a system of evaluating good or bad moments or a simple and easy way to determine the auspiciousness of a particular moment of the day and night respectively.

It can also be understood by the means of Astrology, which shows the celestial condition for 24 hours of any day depending upon Vedic and Stellar Astrology.

When is Choghadiya Good or Bad?
To find good or bad Choghadiya, first, we need to find the planets that rule each of the day's Choghadiya.

Each Choghadiya is influenced by a planet. It is the characteristics of the planet that decides good or bad Choghadiya.

Let us understand how?
The first Choghadiya Muhurt on any day is ruled by the weekday lord. Like on Monday, the first Muhurta time is ruled by the Moon followed by Saturn, Jupiter, Mars, Sun, Venus, Mercury, and last Choghadiya Muhurat will again be ruled by Moon.

Likewise, on Tuesdays, the first Choghadiya will belong to Mars, followed by Sun and so on and the last one will again belong to Mars. In the above examples, we found good or bad Choghadiyas of the day time only.

In Vedic Astrology, Planets are said to have good or bad characteristics.

Choghadiya ruled by Mercury, Moon, Jupiter, and Venus should be preferred for all types of auspicious work because these are soft and auspicious planets.

Choghadiya ruled by Sun, Mars, and Saturn should be avoided as far as possible since these are aggressive planets having harsh and tough effects.

Below is the List of all Choghadiyas with significance.

Moon Rules Amrit Choghadiya

The Moon is a beautiful watery planet, full of thoughts and likes to wander.

Amrit Choghadiya is preferred to Learn and Pray to Gods. It can also be used to travel.

Saturn Rules Kaal Choghadiya

Saturn, the Karmic planet, is widely considered to give negative results. So, the Kaal period should totally be neglected.

Jupiter Rules Shubh Choghadiya

Jupiter, the lord of wealth and wisdom. Shubh Choghadiya, therefore, could help in promoting work that involves money. It can be preferred to do any type of work.

Mars Rules Rog Choghadiya

Mars is warrior, and therefore war and fights started in this period will lead to Victory.

Otherwise, Rog should be avoided for all types of work.

Sun Rules Udveg Choghadiya

Sun is a hot and harsh planet as per Vedic Astrology. It is the King and a symbol of royalty, so any government-related tasks could be completed successfully when it is initiated in Udveg.

Venus Rules Char Choghadiya

The most auspicious planet is Venus and rules entertainment. Marriage, acting, dancing and related careers started in this period will be completed successfully.

Mercury Rules Labh Choghadiya

Mercury, the planet of intellect rules Labh. So, this period should be used to read and write exams, prepare for exams.

CHOGHADIYA LORD AND SUGGESTED ACTIVITIES

Ruling Planet	Muhurta Name	Effect	Works Recommended
Sun	Udveg (Anxiety)	Bad	Government related work
Moon	Amrit (Nectar)	Good	All type of works
Mars	Rog (Illness)	Bad	Attack, War, Fights, Debate
Mercury	Labh (Profit)	Good	Start Business, Education, etc.
Jupiter	Shubh (Auspicious)	Good	Marriage, Religious activities
Venus	Char (Moving)	Good	Travel
Saturn	Kaal (Death)	Bad	Wealth building activities

INTERPRETATION OF 'GOOD' & 'BAD' CHOGHADIYA IN A CHOGHADIYA TABLE

How To Identify Meaning Of Different Choghadiya In A Choghadiya Table?

Choghadiya	Meaning
Amrit	Amrit Choghadiya is the time under the influence of Moon. Moon is considered a beneficial planet in Hindu Vedic Astrology. So, Amrit Choghadiya is regarded as a highly auspicious time in Hindu Astrology. This time is considered beneficial for all types of occasions or work.
Shubh	Shubh Choghadiya is the time under the influence of Jupiter. In Hindu Astrology, Jupiter is a beneficial planet, making it a Shubh Muhurat. Shubh Choghadiya is often taken into account for auspicious occasions, especially for determining marriage dates and conducting marriage ceremonies.
Labh	Labh is a Choghadiya time under the influence of Mercury. Mercury is regarded as a beneficial planet, thus the duration under its influence is considered auspicious. It is an auspicious time but is an exceptionally fruitful time if one wants to start any new learning or acquire new skills or start an education or a course.
Char	Char Choghadiya is associated with the planet Venus. Hindu Astrology considers the influence of Venus quite auspicious. So, the time under its influence, known as Char or Chanchal is often considered for auspicious works. Venus is the planet of movement, so, people look at Char Choghadiya to determine the best time to travel.
Udveg	Udveg Choghadiya is the time under the influence of Sun. In Hindu Vedic Astrology, Sun is a malefic planet and has adverse effects. Thus, it's advisable to avoid auspicious work or new starts during Udveg. However, Udveg Choghadiya is considered to be beneficial in government-related matters.
Kaal	Kaal Choghadiya is associated with the planet Saturn. In Hindu Astrology, Saturn is believed to be a malefic planet and the time under its influence is known as Kaal Choghadiya. No auspicious work should be done during this time. However, if the new work is expected to result in accumulation of wealth or is related to the same, it can be performed during this time.
Rog	Rog Choghadiya is associated with the planet Mars. According to Hindu Vedic Astrology, Mars is not regarded as a beneficial planet. This planet has negative energy and no auspicious work is done during the time under its influence. While falling under the influence of Mars, Rog Choghadiya is often recommended at the time of War, or if one wants to defeat their enemy.

Using **Choghadiya** and **Panchang**, one can find **Daily Choghadiya** as well as **Weekly Choghadiya** along with accurate information on Vaar Vela, Kaal Ratri and Kaal Vela. Use the Daily **Choghadiya table** to find out about the **Shubh Muhurat** in a day. Planning important work with reference to Choghadiya is a way to ensure success and prosperity in every endeavor that you undertake.

3

DAY & NIGHT CHOGHADIYAS

			Din ki Choghadiya				
रवि	सोम	मंगल	बुध	गुरु	शुक्र	शनि	SAMAY
उद्वेग	अमृत	रोग	लाभ	शुभ	चर	काल	6.00 - 7.30
चर	काल	उद्वेग	अमृत	रोग	लाभ	शुभ	7.30 - 9.00
लाभ	शुभ	चर	काल	उद्वेग	अमृत	रोग	9.00 - 10.30
अमृत	रोग	लाभ	शुभ	चर	काल	उद्वेग	10.30 - 12.00
काल	उद्वेग	अमृत	रोग	लाभ	शुभ	चर	12.00 - 1.30
शुभ	चर	काल	उद्वेग	अमृत	रोग	लाभ	1.30 - 3.00
रोग	लाभ	शुभ	चर	काल	उद्वेग	अमृत	3.00 - 4.30
उद्वेग	अमृत	रोग	लाभ	शुभ	चर	काल	4.30 - 6.00

DAY CHOGHADIYA TABLE

Time	Sun	Mon	Tue	Wed	Thu	Fri	Sat
06:00	Udveg	Amrit	Rog	Labh	Subh	Chal	Kaal
07:30	Chal	Kaal	Udveg	Amrit	Rog	Labh	Shubh
09:00	Labh	Shubh	Chal	Kaal	Udveg	Amrit	Rog
10:30	Amrit	Rog	Labh	Shubh	Chal	Kaal	Udveg
12:00	Kaal	Udveg	Amrit	Rog	Labh	Shubh	Chal
13:30	Shubh	Chal	Kaal	Udveg	Amrit	Rog	Labh
15:00	Rog	Labh	Shubh	Chal	Kaal	Udveg	Amrit
16:30	Udveg	Amrit	Rog	Labh	Shubh	Chal	Kaal

Raat ki Choghadiya						
रवि	**सोम**	**मंगल**	**बुध**	**गुरु**	**शुक्र**	**शनि**
शुभ	चर	काल	उद्वेग	अमृत	रोग	लाभ
अमृत	रोग	लाभ	शुभ	चर	काल	उद्वेग
चर	काल	उद्वेग	अमृत	रोग	लाभ	शुभ
रोग	लाभ	शुभ	चर	काल	उद्वेग	अमृत
काल	उद्वेग	अमृत	रोग	लाभ	शुभ	चर
लाभ	शुभ	चर	काल	उद्वेग	अमृत	रोग
उद्वेग	अमृत	रोग	लाभ	शुभ	चर	काल
शुभ	चर	काल	उद्वेग	अमृत	रोग	लाभ

NIGHT CHOGHADIYA TABLE

Time	Sun	Mon	Tue	Wed	Thu	Fri	Sat
18:00	Shubh	Chal	Kaal	Udveg	Amrit	Rog	Labh
19:30	Amrit	Rog	Labh	Shubh	Chal	Kaal	Udveg
21:00	Chal	Kaal	Udveg	Amrit	Rog	Labh	Shubh
22:30	Rog	Labh	Shubh	Chal	Kaal	Udveg	Amrit
00:00	Kaal	Udveg	Amrit	Rog	Labh	Shubh	Chal
01:30	Labh	Shubh	Chal	Kaal	Udveg	Amrit	Rog
03:00	Udveg	Amrit	Rog	Labh	Shubh	Chal	Kaal
04:30	Shubh	Chal	Kaal	Udveg	Amrit	Rog	Labh

ASTROLOGY

1. **ASTROLOGY & ITS PRACTICAL APPROACH**
2. **THE ZODIAC**
3. **THE 12 HOUSES**
4. **THE PLANETS & ITS CORRESPONDING VEDIC MANTRAS**
5. **THE PLANETS – ITS CHARACTERISTICS & PROPERTIES – (TF)**

1

ASTROLOGY & ITS PRACTICAL APPROACH

Introduction to Astrology in Hinduism: Astrology, known as **"Jyotish Shastra"** in Sanskrit, is an ancient system of divination and knowledge that has deep roots in Hinduism. It is the study of the positions and movements of celestial bodies, such as planets and stars, and their influence on human life and natural phenomena. In Hinduism, astrology is considered as a sacred science and is closely intertwined with religious and cultural practices.

Purpose of Astrology in Hinduism: The purpose of astrology in Hinduism is multifaceted:

1. **Guidance:** Astrology is used to provide guidance and insights into various aspects of life, including personal and spiritual development, career, relationships, health, and more.

2. **Timing of Rituals:** Astrology helps in determining auspicious times (Muhurta) for performing important rituals, ceremonies, and events. This ensures that these activities are conducted in alignment with favorable planetary influences.

3. **Karma and Destiny:** Hinduism believes in the concept of Karma, where one's actions in past lives and the present influence their future. Astrology is used to gain insights into one's Karmic patterns and potential life paths.

4. **Spiritual Growth:** Astrology is used as a tool for spiritual growth and self-awareness. It can help individuals to understand their strengths, weaknesses, and spiritual purpose.

Relevance of Astrology in Hinduism: Astrology is highly relevant in Hinduism for several reasons:

1. **Cultural Tradition:** Astrology has been an integral part of Hindu culture for centuries. It is deeply embedded in daily life, religious ceremonies, and festivals.

2. **Religious Ceremonies:** Astrology plays a crucial role in determining the most auspicious times for religious ceremonies, such as weddings, pujas (prayers), yagnas (fire rituals), and temple consecrations.

3. **Personal and Professional Life:** Many Hindus consult astrologers for guidance on important life decisions, career choices, financial investments, and other significant matters.

4. **Spiritual Significance:** Astrology is seen as a means of understanding the divine plan and cosmic order. It aids in connecting with the cosmic energies and aligning one's life with spiritual principles.

Application of Astrology in Hinduism: Astrology is applied in various ways within Hinduism:

1. **Birth Chart (Kundali):** Every individual's birth chart, known as **"kundali,"** is created based on their date, time, and place of birth. The kundali provides insights into one's personality, life path, and potential challenges and opportunities.

2. **Muhurta:** Astrologers are consulted to determine auspicious times for various activities, such as weddings, housewarming ceremonies, and business ventures.

3. **Astrological Remedies:** Astrology offers remedies to mitigate challenging planetary influences. These remedies may include wearing specific gemstones, performing rituals, chanting mantras, and observing fasting.

4. **Spiritual Guidance:** Astrology is used for spiritual guidance and self-discovery. It can help individuals align with their spiritual path and purpose.

5. **Forecasting:** Astrologers provide forecasts and predictions for individuals and nations, which can influence decision-making.

It's important to note that while astrology is an integral part of Hinduism, interpretations and practices may vary among individuals and astrologers. Some view astrology as a science, while others see it as a spiritual and philosophical tool. Ultimately, the relevance and application of astrology in Hinduism are deeply rooted in cultural and religious traditions and personal beliefs.

A PRACTICAL APPROACH TO ASTROLOGY

By knowing what our destiny indicates and by knowing what pitfalls lie ahead of us, and the courses which threaten disaster, we can exercise our choice to determine the best course to avert the catastrophe.

"To be forewarned is to be forearmed".

The horoscope indicates the pattern on which life is built. The stars indicate what will come to pass, but with intelligence and free will one can change the natural course of events also.

Astrology points out the potentialities, capabilities and limitations of the individual.

Astrology shows the way and it is for us to decide whether we have to follow the path and maintain a balance between the mental and the physical aspects of ourselves.

Astrology points out the weak spots in our character and shows us the reason why we are not successful in our endeavours in life. When we are in danger of suffering due to our weaknesses and when misfortune is likely to overtake us, **Astrology gives us a forewarning.**

An astrological birth chart reflects the zodiac condition governing the time of birth. **It consists of 9 planets (grahas) and 12 houses (sthanas).** The position of different planets in various houses or grahabasthana is referred to as the planetary structure of a specific astrological birth chart. According to astrological belief and culture, an individual's life and destiny is thoroughly governed by the position and strengths of the planets as calculated and expounded in an astrological chart.

Astrology is a perfect combination of art and science which offers different mathematical instrument in order to interpret the influences of different grahas on the overall life and destiny of an individual. Referred to as a **Divine Science**, astrology aids us in obtaining a valuable reflection of future life.

Astrology can only indicate what is likely to happen, but no astrologer is qualified to determine how the events which are preordained shall influence each individual. This depends on the individual's own free will and the degree of development he has attained and which will determine his mental attitude towards anything which may happen. One can hope to receive results through one's opportunities in proportion to the use one makes of them.

Astrology points out the best and shortest and safest route to a given goal. It offers solutions to our problems. It reveals us to ourselves-our physical and psychical make up, our tendencies and our possibilities.

Astrology makes it possible for us to analyse and diagnose ourselves. And with the help of Astrology, we may use our intelligence and free will both to avert dangers and to convert opportunity to our advantage.

Astrology is the emancipator from ignorance which helps the individual to understand himself, and also to understand one's fellowmen better, and to be more sympathetic and more tolerant.

Indian Vedic astrology is a vast subject which includes a wide array of segments such as palm reading, astrological birth chart reading, horoscope reading, face reading, varsha phala or annual prediction and many others. Many astrologers and astrologists consider astrological birth chart reading as the most effective tool for prediction since it involves birth time of the particular individual concerned.

Astrology can offer help to human being in many facets of daily life such as health management, business success, professional stability, success in conjugal life, offspring academic and behavior related problem solving, realizing own strengths and weaknesses, understanding skills, favorable and unfavorable time in life etc.

In short, by taking the advantage of astrology and astrological instruments one can enjoy the life at its fullest extent and become able to make many informed decisions regarding several life activities and opportunities.

Frequently Asked Questions:
Is Astrology a Science?
The answer is yes. It is basically **a science of time.** Every moment in time has a certain meaning, quality or significance attached to it. By being born at a particular moment in time as per astronomical chart, we imbibe this quality. Personal horoscope is our guide map for our journey through time on earth. It is believed that studying astrological chart or preparing birth chart involves great deal of astronomy and its interpretation is based on certain recognised rules. A birth chart contains different combinations of planets to describe various situations in life, which include mental and physical abilities, profession, partnerships, marriage, children, and difficulties and so on.

Modern Astrology Hypothesis
- A birth chart reveals our potential and what we can aim for.
- The symbols in a birth chart have to be decoded.
- All the viewpoints in the whole chart are connected with the planetary movements of the present time.

Why is Astrology Important?

The astrological birth chart of every one of us is independent of individual opinions. There are many instances in our lives when we arrive at the comparison mode of thinking though we know comparison is not good. Sometimes, we ask ourselves, "Why am I doing this? What is happening in my life? Why do I have to see this?" And so on. It is here that astrology brings a new opinion in our lives. Astrology does not mean we have to be solely dependent on fate. It lays emphasis on our karma and actions as astrology firmly believes in, **"Today's karma is tomorrow's fate"**.

Astrology lights the path known as life and it is entirely our choice as to whether we want to travel on this path or not. Astrology helps us to know how we can make the best possible use of these tools in our lives for our benefit when we see the bad phase in our lives. Astrology is the connecting chord among our past, present and future. It knows no caste, religion, gender or nationality. It simply concerns the important fundamentals of our everyday lives.

2

THE ZODIAC

The Zodiac system, often referred to as the zodiac signs or astrological signs, is a widely recognized and influential concept in Astrology. It divides the celestial belt into twelve distinct signs, each associated with specific personality traits, characteristics, and tendencies.

Astrologers interpret these signs based on the position of the Sun at the time of a person's birth.

Zodiac signs are often used to create individual birth charts or horoscopes, which provide insights into a person's potential life path, behaviour, and challenges.

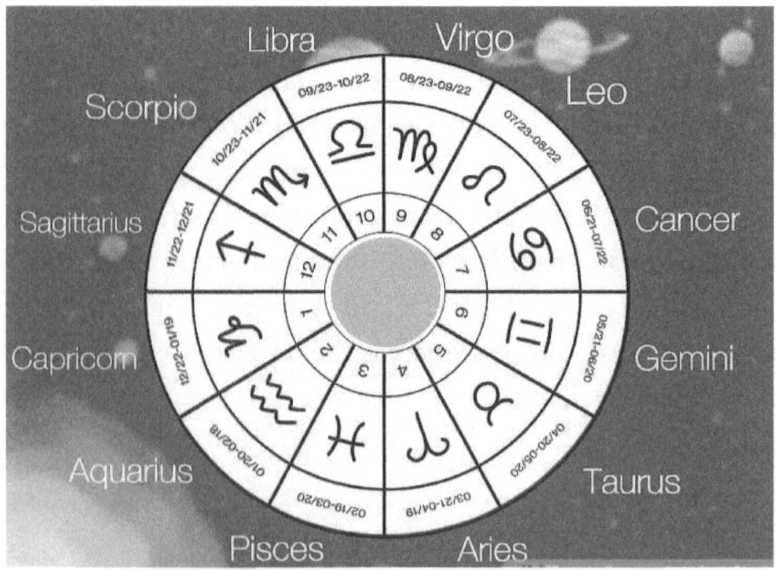

The Zodiac is circular in shape, and the circumference of the Zodiacal belt contains 360 degrees; consequently, each house or sign contains thirty degrees. The twelve equal parts, called signs of the Zodiac, are represented, by imaginary figures, and they affect the body, the character, the disposition and the mental and moral attributes, as well as possibilities for success or failure of a human being.

The twelve signs, which are also called houses, describe the environment and circumstances, the possibilities and limitations of every phase of destiny with which each individual is confronted in his voyage through life.

The houses of the Zodiac are represented by the chart in a horoscope. In order to determine the importance and strength any particular house, it is necessary to examine, first, the lord of that house and its aspects.

These signs are associated with the positions of various celestial bodies, including the Sun, Moon, and planets, at the time of a person's birth. Each sign represents certain traits, characteristics, and influences on an individual's personality and life.

THE COMPONENTS OF THE ZODIAC SYSTEM:

The Zodiac system consists of the following key components:

i. **Twelve Zodiac Signs:** There are twelve **Zodiac Signs –** **(ZS)** – [{It refers to one of 12 specific constellations of the zodiac that the sun passes through} means, a person's particular sign of the zodiac is one that the sun was 'IN' when they were born], each representing a specific period of the year. The signs, in order are as – Aries, Taurus, Gemini, Cancer, Leo, Virgo, Libra, Scorpio, Sagittarius, Capricorn, Aquarius, and Pisces.

	ZS – English names	*ZS – Hindi names*	*ZS – Period – (Time span)*
1.	**ARIES** – the Ram	**MESH**	(March 21 – April 19)
2.	**TAURUS** – the Bull	**VRISABH**	(April 20 – May 20)
3.	**GEMINI** – the Twins	**MITHUN**	(May 21 – June 20)
4.	**CANCER** – the Crab	**KARK**	(June 21 – July 22)
5.	**LEO** – the Lion	**SIMHA**	(July 23 – August 22)
6.	**VIRGO** – the Virgin	**KANYA**	(August 23 – September 22)
7.	**LIBRA** – the Balance	**TULA**	(September 23 – October 22)
8.	**SCORPIO** – the Scorpion	**VRISCHIK**	(October 23 – November 21)
9.	**SAGITTARIUS** – the Archer	**DHANU**	(November22 – December21)
10.	**CAPRICORN** – the Goat	**MAKAR**	(December 22 – January 19)
11.	**AQUARIUS** – the Water Carrier	**KUMBHA**	(January 20 – February 18)
12.	**PISCES** – the Fish	**MEEN**	(February 19 – March 20)

ii. **Elements:** The twelve signs are grouped into four elements, each associated with specific traits and characteristics.

1. **Fire Signs:** Aries, Leo, Sagittarius (associated with energy, enthusiasm, and assertiveness).

2. **Earth Signs:** Taurus, Virgo, Capricorn (associated with practicality, stability, and grounded ness).

3. **Air Signs:** Gemini, Libra, Aquarius (associated with communication, intellect, and social relationships).

4. **Water Signs:** Cancer, Scorpio, Pisces (associated with emotions, intuition, and sensitivity).

iii. **Ruling Planets:** Each sign is associated with a ruling planet, which is believed to influence its characteristics and qualities.

	Zodiac Signs		_Ruling Planet_
1.	Aries	–	Mars
2.	Taurus	–	Venus
3.	Gemini	–	Mercury
4.	Cancer	–	Moon
5.	Leo	–	Sun
6.	Virgo	–	Mercury
7.	Libra	–	Venus
8.	Scorpio	–	Mars (Traditional), Pluto (Modern)
9.	Sagittarius	–	Jupiter
10.	Capricorn	–	Saturn
11.	Aquarius	–	Saturn (Traditional), Uranus (Modern)
12.	Pisces	–	Jupiter (Traditional), Neptune (Modern)

iv. **Modalities:** The twelve signs are further categorized into three modalities – (a particular mode in which it exists, experienced or expressed), representing different approaches to life and change.

1. **Cardinal Signs:** Aries, Cancer, Libra, Capricorn (associated with leadership and initiating change).

2. **Fixed Signs:** Taurus, Leo, Scorpio, Aquarius (associated with stability and determination).

3. **Mutable Signs:** Gemini, Virgo, Sagittarius, Pisces (associated with adaptability and flexibility).

Components of the zodiac system with their signs & symbols in a tabulated pictorial view

The Signs and Their Rulers	
Sign	**Planetary Ruler**
♈ Aries	♂ Mars
♉ Taurus	♀ Venus
♊ Gemini	☿ Mercury
♋ Cancer	☽ Moon
♌ Leo	☉ Sun
♍ Virgo	☿ Mercury
♎ Libra	♀ Venus
♏ Scorpio	♇ Pluto
♐ Sagittarius	♃ Jupiter
♑ Capricorn	♄ Saturn
♒ Aquarius	♅ Uranus
♓ Pisces	♆ Neptune

Aries		♈
Taurus		♉
Gemini		♊
Cancer		♋
Leo		♌
Virgo		♍
Libra		♎
Scorpio		♏
Sagittarius		♐
Capricorn		♑
Aquarius		♒
Pisces		♓

These components together form the basis of the Zodiac system in astrology, and astrologers use them to provide insights into a person's personality, relationships, career, and various other aspects of life based on their birth chart and the positions of celestial bodies at the time of their birth.

THE TWELVE HOUSES

When a person is born, or an incident occurs, at a certain point or degree of one of the twelve signs of the Zodiac will be rising on the Eastern horizon. This rising sign is called the **Ascendant**, and in the Hindu system it is known as the **Lagna**.

The character of a person and also the course of his life will largely depend upon this rising sign. In order to determine the first house, or the rising sign, the exact hour of birth is very necessary. The lack of accuracy of the time of birth, may result in errors of judgement in diagnosing a horoscope. Even a slight absence of harmony may interfere with the perfect operation of a powerful configuration. **The horoscope is a chart indicating the positions of the sun, the moon and seven planets in relation to the earth and the Zodiac for any given moment of time.**

The twelve houses of the horoscope that govern a man's life, in its different aspects are as follows:

THE 12 HOUSES OF AN ASTROLOGICAL HOROSCOPE CHART & ITS DEFINATION & INTERPRETATION

In astrology, the birth chart is divided into 12 houses, each representing different aspects of a person's life and experiences.

These houses are determined by the exact time and location of a person's birth. Each house has its unique significance and influences the interpretation of a person's personality, relationships, career, and various other areas of life. Here is a brief interpretation of each house in astrology:

1. **First House (Ascendant or "Self"):**
   - The first house is **Aries – ruled by Mars.**
   - **Represents:** Self, personality, physical appearance, overall approach to life.
   - **Interpretation:** The first house reveals how you present yourself to the world, your self-image, and how others perceive you. It represents your outlook on life, personal identity, and physical vitality.

2. **Second House ("Possessions and Values"):**
   - The second house is **Taurus – ruled by Venus.**
   - **Represents:** Finances, material possessions, values, self-worth.
   - **Interpretation:** The second house is related to your attitude towards money, personal values, and how you handle financial matters. It also indicates your relationship with material possessions and how you derive a sense of self-worth.

3. **Third House ("Communication and Siblings"):**
   - The third house is **Gemini – ruled by Mercury.**
   - **Represents:** Communication, short trips, siblings, early education.
   - **Interpretation:** The third house relates to communication skills, learning, and interactions with siblings and neighbours. It reflects your

curiosity, adaptability, and how you express your ideas.

4. **Fourth House ("Home and Family"):**
   - The fourth house is **Cancer – ruled by the moon.**
   - **Represents:** Home, family, roots, inner emotions.
   - **Interpretation:** The fourth house is associated with your home life, family relationships and emotional foundation. It also signifies your private life and the sense of security and comfort you seek.

5. **Fifth House ("Creativity and Romance"):**
   - The fifth house is **Leo – ruled over by the Sun.**
   - **Represents:** Creativity, self-expression, love affairs, children.
   - **Interpretation:** The fifth house represents creative pursuits, love affairs, and matters related to children. It also indicates how you express yourself creatively and how you find joy and pleasure.

6. **Sixth House ("Health and Work"):**
   - The sixth house is **Virgo – ruled over by Mercury**
   - **Represents:** Health, work, service, routines.
   - **Interpretation:** The sixth house is connected to daily routines, health, and work environment. It represents your approach to work, service to others, and attention to physical well-being.

7. **Seventh House ("Partnerships and Marriage"):**
   - The seventh house is **Libra – ruled over by Venus.**
   - **Represents:** Partnerships, marriage, significant others.
   - **Interpretation:** The seventh house is about one-on-one relationships, including romantic partners

and business partnerships. It reflects your approach to collaboration and the qualities you seek in a partner.

8. **Eighth House ("Transformation and Shared Resources"):**
   - The eighth house is **Scorpio – ruled over by Mars.**
   - **Represents:** Transformation, shared resources, sexuality.
   - **Interpretation:** The eighth house is associated with deep transformation, shared resources, and intimacy. It also relates to issues of life and death, inheritance, and matters beyond the material realm.

9. **Ninth House ("Philosophy and Higher Learning"):**
   - The ninth house is **Sagittarius – ruled over by Jupiter**.
   - **Represents:** Higher education, travel, philosophy, beliefs.
   - **Interpretation:** The ninth house is connected to higher education, travel, and philosophical beliefs. It reflects your spiritual inclinations, higher learning, and search for meaning in life.

10. **Tenth House ("Career and Public Image"):**
   - The tenth house is **Capricorn – ruled over by Saturn**
   - **Represents:** Career, public image, achievements, authority.
   - **Interpretation:** The tenth house signifies your career, professional achievements, and public reputation. It reflects your ambition, sense of

responsibility, and how you relate to authority figures.

11. **Eleventh House ("Friendships and Aspirations"):**
    - The eleventh house is **Aquarius – ruled over by Uranus.**
    - **Represents:** Friendships, social circles, hopes, dreams.
    - **Interpretation:** The eleventh house is about social connections, friendships, and collective aspirations. It reflects your involvement in group activities, humanitarian interests, and long-term goals.

12. **Twelfth House ("Spirituality and Subconscious"):**
    - The twelfth house is **Pisces – ruled over by Neptune.**
    - **Represents:** Spirituality, subconscious, hidden matters.
    - **Interpretation:** The twelfth house is associated with spirituality, hidden aspects of life, and the subconscious mind. It reflects your capacity for introspection, involvement in charitable activities, and connection with the divine.

Astrologers analyse the planets and signs placed in each house, as well as their aspects to other planets, to gain deeper insights into a person's life and experiences. The interpretation of the houses is an essential part of constructing a comprehensive and detailed astrological profile for an individual.

THE 12 HOUSES – Represented & Interpreted in Pictorial Format – Simplified & Co-Related for Clear Understanding.

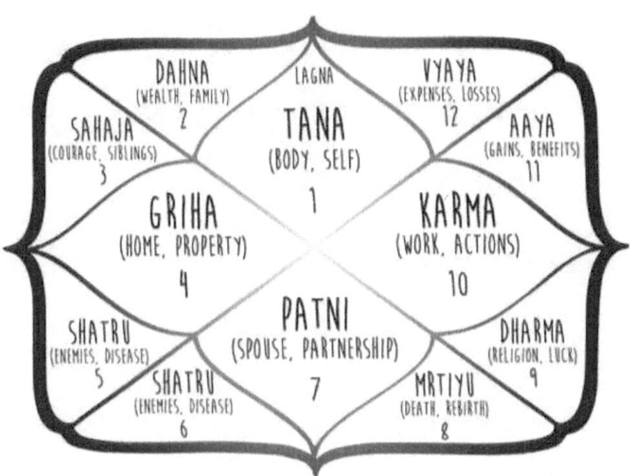

DAHNA
(WEALTH, FAMILY)
2
LAGNA
VYAYA
(EXPENSES, LOSSES)
12
SAHAJA
(COURAGE, SIBLINGS)
3
TANA
(BODY, SELF)
1
AAYA
(GAINS, BENEFITS)
11
GRIHA
(HOME, PROPERTY)
4
KARMA
(WORK, ACTIONS)
10
SHATRU
(ENEMIES, DISEASE)
5
PATNI
(SPOUSE, PARTNERSHIP)
7
DHARMA
(RELIGION, LUCK)
9
SHATRU
(ENEMIES, DISEASE)
6
MRTIYU
(DEATH, REBIRTH)
8

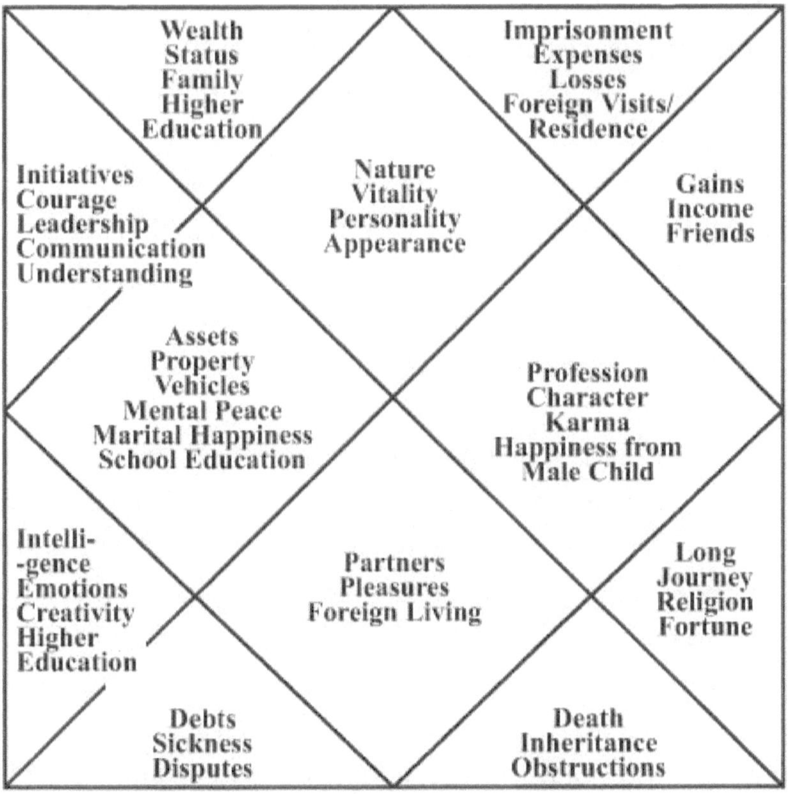

Wealth
Status
Family
Higher
Education
Imprisonment
Expenses
Losses
Foreign Visits/
Residence
Initiatives
Courage
Leadership
Communication
Understanding
Nature
Vitality
Personality
Appearance
Gains
Income
Friends
Assets
Property
Vehicles
Mental Peace
Marital Happiness
School Education
Profession
Character
Karma
Happiness from
Male Child
Intelli-
-gence
Emotions
Creativity
Higher
Education
Partners
Pleasures
Foreign Living
Long
Journey
Religion
Fortune
Debts
Sickness
Disputes
Death
Inheritance
Obstructions

4

THE PLANETS & ITS CORRESPONDING VEDIC MANTRAS

Mantras bring healing and harmony to our body, mind and soul. According to our ancient seers, there are 108 sound frequencies in the universe based on the movement of planets in the cosmos. (12 zodiac signs x 9 planets). With the power of mantras, we are able to connect with the frequency of the Cosmos.

The 9 planets (Sun, Moon, Mars, Mercury, Jupiter, Venus, Saturn, Rahu, Ketu) have 108 names each. And these names are expressed as Mantras to connect deeply with the planets. This is the safest and best remedy that we can do to amplify the positive effects and nullify the negative effects of the planets.

Out of the 108 mantras – one mantra each for one planet becomes our personal mantra based on our Vedic birth chart. Our personal mantra will help us to connect with the energy of the planet and with continuous practice the planets will reveal some secrets underlying its purpose in our birth chart.

For better health we can chant mantra of the planet that rules our first house. For a calm and peaceful state of mind we can chant the mantra of the moon. For relationship problems we can chant the mantra of the planet that rules our 7th house and so on.

The Beej Mantras of Nine Planets (Navagraha) are very useful in the Dasha's of any planet. By reciting these Navagraha Beej mantras, we can eliminate all the evil effects of the planets.

BENEFITS OF CHANTING NAVGRAHA MANTRAS

- Chanting Navgraha Beej mantras is highly beneficial in promoting the overall well-being of the individual. By chanting all of these mantras regularly, we can ease the malefic effects of the nine planets in our horoscope.
- Chant the prescribed mantra as per our horoscope and we will see a marked difference within a period of 40 days.
- The Navagraha mantra chosen as per the horoscope of the individual helps to strengthen the positive impact of the said planet and mitigate the negative effects.
- It helps to overcome Navagraha doshas and attain peace and happiness in life.
- It keeps bad luck and misfortune at bay
- It prevents diseases and ailments
- It significantly improves the quality of personal as well as professional life

- For best results, using the rosary made of the Rashi stone (Astro-Gemstone) of that particular planet is advisable. For example, use a pearl rosary for Chandra mantra and a coral rosary for Mars mantra and so on.

The Beej Mantras of Nine Planets (Navagraha) are very useful in the Dasha's of any planet. By reciting these Navagraha Beej mantras, we can eliminate all the evil effects of the planets.

Surya Beej Mantra

ॐ ह्रां ह्रीं ह्रौं सः सूर्याय नमः ।

Om hraam hreem hraum sah suryaaya namah

Chandra Beej Mantra

ॐ श्रां श्रीं श्रौं सः चंद्राय नमः ।

Om shraam shreem shroum sah chandraya namah

Mangal Beej Mantra

ॐ क्रां क्रीं क्रौं सः भौमाय नमः ।

Om kraam kreem kraum sah bhaumaya namah

Buddha Beej Mantra

ॐ ब्रां ब्रीं ब्रौं सः बुधाय नमः।

Om braam breem braum sah budhaaya namah

Brihaspati Beej Mantra

ॐ ग्रां ग्रीं ग्रौं सः गुरूवे नमः ।

Om graam greem graum sah gurave namah

Shukra Beej Mantra

ॐ द्रां द्रीं द्रौं सः शुक्राय नमः ।

Om draam dreem draum sah shukraya namah

Shani Beej Mantra

ॐ प्रां प्रीं प्रौं सः शनैश्चराय नमः ।

Om praam preem praum sah shanaishcharaaya namah

Rahu Beej Mantra

ॐ भ्रां भ्रीं भ्रौं सः राहवे नमः ।

Om bhraam bhreem bhraum sah rahave namah

Ketu Beej Mantra

ॐ स्रां स्रीं स्रौं सः केतवे नमः ।

Om sraam sreem sraum sah ketave namah

THE PLANETS – ITS CHARACTERISTICS & PROPERTIES – (TF)

Tabulated formats of the Planets represented Daywise with its coressponding Sunsign interpretating the Characteristics & Properties.

		1	2	3
SR.	**DAYS**	**PLANET E / H**	**PLANET SYMBOL**	**PLANET TATWA**
1	SUNDAY	SUN / RAVI	Sun	FIRE
2	MONDAY	MOON / CHANDRA	Moon	WATER
3	TUESDAY	MARS / MANGAL	Mars	FIRE
4	WEDNESDAY	MERCURY/ BUDHA	MERCURY	EARTH
5	THURSDAY	JUPITER / GURU	JUPITER	SKY
6	FRIDAY	VENUS / SHUKRA	Venus	WATER
7	SATURDAY	SATURN / SHANI	Saturn	AIR

4	5	6	7
PLANET COLOUR	**PLANET QUALITY**	**PLANET GOVERNANCE**	**PLANET FUNCTION**
BRIGHT RED	CREATIVE ENERGY	SOUL	NOBILITY
MILKY WHITE	HEART	MIND	EMOTION
DARK RED	POWER	STRENGTH	ADMINISTRATION
GREEN	EDUCATION	SPEECH	INTELLIGENCE
LEMON YELLOW	KNOWLEDGE	KNOWLEDGE	RELIGION
MIXED COLOUR	ART	SEMEN	BEAUTY
BLUE BLACK	EXPERIENCE	SORROW	DELAY

SR.	DAYS	8 PLANET FEATURES	9 SUN SIGN E / H	10 SUN SIGN SYMBOL
1	SUNDAY	Truth, Nobility, Status, Literature	LEO / SINHA	Leo
2	MONDAY	Emotional, Sensitive, Beauty, Variable Mind.	CANCER / KARK	CANCER
3	TUESDAY	Aggressiveness, Determination, Activity, Hostile.	ARIES / MESH	Aries
4	WEDNESDAY	Intelligence, Perfection, Systematic Thinking, Criticism and Analysis.	GEMINI / MITHUN	GEMINI
5	THURSDAY	Religious, Wisdom, Experience, Vision, Judgement, Foresight, Philanthropy.	SAGITTARIUS DHANU	Sagittarius
6	FRIDAY	Beauty, Sophistication, Culture, Good looks, Good Nature. Talent	LIBRA / TULA	Libra
7	SATURDAY	Delay, Constrains, Suffering, Experience, Maturity	AQUARIUS / KUMBHA	Aquarius

11	12	13
SUN SIGN LORD	**SUN SIGN PERIOD**	**SUN SIGN FEATURES**
LEO	JUL 22 – AUG 21	Leadership qualities, Very powerful sign.
CANCER	JUNE 21 – JULY 21	Very emotional, Highly sensitive.
ARIES SCORPIO	MAR 20 – APR 18 OCT 22 – NOV 21	Forcefull / 3S – Suspicious, Secretive, Sexy.
GEMINI VIRGO	MAY 20 – JUN 20 AUG 22 – SEPT 20	Dual Mind / 3P – Purity, Perfection, Practicality.
SAGITTARIUS PISCES	NOV 22 – DEC 22 FEB 18 – MAR 19	Ambitious, Very Good, Flies high / Flexible / Intutitional, Emotional and Good Advisers.
LIBRA TAURAS	SEP 20 – OCT 22 APR 19 – MAY 20	Stubborn / Balanced
AQUARIUS CAPRICORN	JAN 20 – FEB 18 DEC 23 – JAN 19	Practical, Nice people, but can be fooled easily/ Flexible, Go-advising to situation, Capable of Option.

SR.	DAYS	14 STRONG	15 DETRIMENT	16 EXALTATION
1	SUNDAY	SCORPIO	AQUARIES	ARIES
2	MONDAY	–	CAPRICORN	TAURAS
3	TUESDAY	LEO	LIBRA & TAURAS	CAPRICORN
4	WEDNESDAY	CANCER & CAPRICORN	SAGITTARIUS & PISCES	VIRGO
5	THURSDAY	TAURAS & LIBRA	GEMINI & VIRGO	CANCER
6	FRIDAY	SAGITTARIUS	SCORPIA & ARIES	PISCES
7	SATURDAY	GEMINI & VIRGO	CANCER & LEO	LIBRA

17	18	19	20
FALL	FRIENDS	ENEMIES	NEUTRAL
LIBRA	MOON MARS JUPITER	VENUS SATURN	MERCURY
SCORPIA	SUN MERCURY	NONE	MARS JUPITER VENUS SATURN
CANCER	SUN MOON JUPITER	MERCURY	SATURN VENUS
LEO	SUN VENUS	MOON	SATURN MARS JUPITER
CAPRICORN	SUN MOON MARS	MARS VENUS	SATURN
VIRGO	MARS VENUS	SUN MOON MARS	JUPITER
ARIES	MERCURY SATURN	SUN MOON	MARS JUPITER

GEMOLOGY

1

INTRODUCTION

Gemstones are usually inorganic minerals that occur naturally in the earth's crust and are extracted, cut and polished to be used for various purposes. Gemstones are known for their beauty and durability.

The Science of Planetary Gemmology is one that has been used in accordance with Astrology for thousands of years. It is the science of understanding how Gemstones transmit and reflect planetary rays, and how they increase planetary influences in a person's life.

Different Gemstones are said to receive their potencies from the Cosmic energies of various planets as depicted below:

Planets	Gemstones	Image
Ravi (Sun)	Ruby	
Chandra (Moon)	Pearl	
Kuja (Mars)	Coral	
Budha (Mercury)	Emerald	
Guru (Jupiter)	Yellow Sapphire	
Sukra (Venus)	Diamond	
Sani (Saturn)	Blue Sapphire	
Rahu (Dragon's Head)	Gomed	
Ketu (Dragon's Tail)	Cat's Eye	

- Vedic astrology and the Ayurveda system of medicine tell us that certain planets can have effects on bodily organs and parts of the body. The planets are also said to have effects on our minds and subtle parts of our consciousness. In addition, their specific positions in the horoscope indicate (to a duly qualified practitioner of this great science) the path of destiny.

- There is a school of thought wherein some astrologers posit that wearing a gem for a planet which causes suffering due to unfortunate positioning at the time of a person's birth will **"propitiate"** that planet or cause it to give less trouble.

- Natural Gems decrease or increase the planet's energy, i.e., the impact of positive & negative energy from its Cosmic rays, if worn during the benefice & malefice period of that particular planet in relation with the planetary corresponding gem with proper orientation, it impacts with a positive effect that makes an individual feel better and elevates his/her confidence.

- Therefore, recommendation of any gem must be given a great deal of concentrated thought by the Astrologer in order to determine whether a gemstone will truly have a positive effect on or not.

- Mistakes can be costly if malefic cosmic rays are unintentionally increased. Therefore, it is only sensible that a conscientious Astrologer who recommends gems to his or her clients will carefully study the science of planetary gemmology in order to correctly prescribe gems.

- This is not a science that can be used only by Vedic Astrologers. Western astrologers can also learn planetary gemmology in order to give viable remedial measures to their clients for mitigating or lessening malefic influences and increasing benefice influences. This is achieved by strengthening planets that can counteract certain rays that are causing problems, or by strengthening planets that rule positive areas of life but are simply weakened due to their placement in the horoscope.

VALUE OF GEMSTONE

The value of Gemstones basically depends on the 4C'S – Colour, Cut, Clarity & Carat.

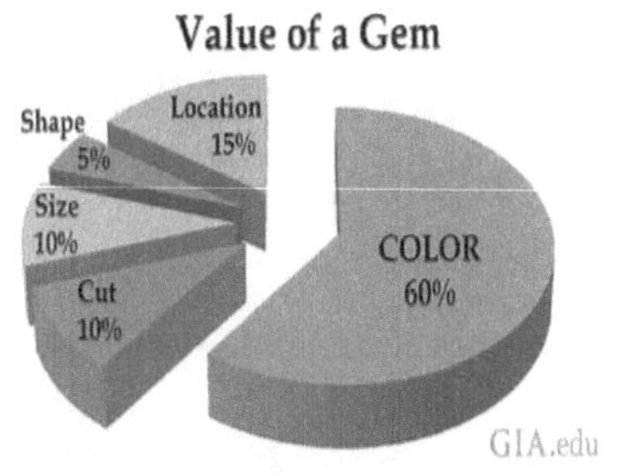

1. **Colour:** The colour of a gemstone is one of its most important characteristics. Different colours are associated with various qualities and energies. For example, red is often associated with passion and energy, while blue represents calm and communication.

2. **Cut:** The way a gemstone is cut affects its brilliance and overall appearance. A well-cut gemstone will sparkle and reflect light beautifully.

3. **Clarity:** Clarity refers to the presence of internal or external flaws, called inclusions and blemishes. Greater clarity often increases a gemstone's value.

4. **Carat Weight:** Carat weight measures the size of a gemstone. Larger gemstones are generally rarer and more valuable, but other factors like colour and clarity also play a role in determining its value.

5. **Origin:** The geographic origin of a gemstone can impact its value and desirability. Certain regions are known for producing gemstones of exceptional quality.

RELEVANCE, INTERPRETATION AND APPLICATION OF GEMSTONES

Gemstones have been used in Astrology for centuries, and their relevance, interpretation, and application in Astrological practices are significant. In Vedic Astrology, specific Gemstones are associated with each of the nine planets (Navagraha's), and these Gemstones are believed to have a direct influence on an individual's life and destiny.

RELEVANCE OF GEMSTONES IN ASTROLOGY:

1. **Planetary Influence:** In Vedic astrology, each planet is associated with specific qualities, energies, and influences on an individual's life. Gemstones are considered conduits for these planetary energies and are used to strengthen or mitigate the effects of specific planets in one's birth chart.

2. **Karmic Remedies:** Astrologers often recommend gemstones as remedies for individuals experiencing challenges or negative planetary influences. Wearing the appropriate gemstone is believed to balance and harmonize the planetary energies, leading to positive changes in one's life.

3. **Alignment with Birth Chart:** The selection of a gemstone is based on an individual's birth chart **(Kundali),** which provides information about the positions of the planets at the time of birth. Gemstones are chosen to align with the positions of benefice or malefic planets in the chart.

INTERPRETATION OF GEMSTONES IN ASTROLOGY:

1. **Specific Gemstone-Planet Associations:** Each planet is associated with a specific gemstone. For example:
   - Ruby (Manikya) is associated with the Sun (Surya).
   - Pearl (Moti) is associated with the Moon (Chandra).
   - Yellow Sapphire (Pukhraj) is associated with Jupiter (Brihaspati).

2. **Planetary Qualities:** The qualities and characteristics of each planet are believed to be reflected in the gemstone. For instance, the Sun is associated with leadership and vitality, so wearing a ruby may enhance these qualities.

3. **Colour and Energy:** The colour of the gemstone is often aligned with the associated planet. For example, the red colour of a ruby corresponds to the Sun's energy, while the blue of a sapphire aligns with Saturn's energy.

APPLICATION OF GEMSTONES IN ASTROLOGY:

1. **Wearing Gemstones:** Individuals are advised to wear the specific gemstone associated with their beneficial planets based on their birth charts. These gemstones are typically worn as jewellery, such as rings, pendants, or bracelets.

2. **Timing:** Gemstones are often recommended during specific planetary periods (dasha's) or when individuals are going through challenging phases in life. Astrologers may suggest wearing gemstones to enhance positive influences or mitigate negative ones.

3. **Purification and Activation:** Before wearing a gemstone, it is purified and activated through specific rituals and mantras to connect it with the planetary energies.

4. **Regular Maintenance:** To maintain the effectiveness of gemstones, individuals may need to cleanse and recharge them periodically.

5. **Consultation with an Astrologer:** The selection of gemstones and their proper use in astrology requires consultation with an experienced astrologer who can analyse an individual's birth chart and recommend the most suitable gemstones.

It's important to note that the effectiveness of gemstones in astrology is a matter of belief and faith. While many individuals find value in astrological gemstones, others may view them sceptically. Astrology, including the use of gemstones, is deeply rooted in cultural and spiritual traditions and varies widely among practitioners and belief systems.

2

ASTRO-GEMOLOGY

INTRODUCTION

Gemmology i.e., the "study (ethnic or scientific) of gemstones, has been an essential branch of applied astrology from the time immemorial

The connection between gemstones and astrology was first identified by the Vedic astrologers. They believed that each gemstone is ruled by a planet and if we could identify the position of planet in each person's chart, and the planetary rulership of a gemstone, gems can be used for personal development, healing and for attracting positive energies.

It is believed that every living being produces some energy in the world. It is this energy field where our emotions, habits, beliefs and thought patterns reside. Gems are thought to affect these energy fields and create an impact on a person's mental and emotional energies. With time, these subtle effects of gems can cause long term changes in a person's habits, emotions, thoughts etc.

However, to gain the benefits of gems, it is crucial that we use the right gemstone according to our ruling planet and horoscope chart. Since only experienced astrologers can understand the complex details associated with planets, their movements, relationships etc. we can rely on them, because not many people understand the idea of ruling planet and can interpret the horoscope chart for which they have used the horoscope system for gemstones recommendations.

GEMSTONES AND ASTROLOGY – THE CONNECTION

Astrology and gemology are two interconnected fields that have been traditionally linked in various cultures, especially in the context of Vedic astrology. The connection between these two fields lies in the belief that specific gemstones can have astrological significance and influence a person's life based on the positions of celestial bodies. Here's an overview of their connection and relevance:

1. **Astrological Significance of Gemstones:** In astrology, it is believed that different planets have specific energies and influences that affect various aspects of a person's life. Gemstones are associated with these planets and are thought to amplify or balance their energies. The idea is that wearing a gemstone associated with a particular planet can strengthen its positive effects and mitigate negative influences.

2. **Planetary Gemology:** Planetary gemology is a branch of gemology that focuses on the use of gemstones for astrological purposes. Different gemstones are associated with specific planets based on their color, composition, and energetic properties. For example, red coral is linked to Mars, blue sapphire to Saturn, and so on.

3. **Remedial Measures:** Astrological gemology is often used as a remedy in Vedic astrology to counteract

challenging planetary influences in a person's birth chart. It is believed that wearing the appropriate gemstone can help harmonize planetary energies and bring positive changes in areas like health, career, relationships, and overall well-being.

4. **Individual's Energetic Alignment:** Proponents of astrological gemology believe that each individual has a unique energetic makeup that is influenced by their birth chart. Wearing a gemstone associated with favourable planets can enhance a person's natural strengths and qualities.

5. **Cultural and Traditional Significance:** The connection between astrology and gemology is deeply rooted in cultural and spiritual traditions. Many cultures, including Vedic and Western astrology, have assigned specific gemstones to planets based on ancient teachings and beliefs.

Relevance: The relevance of the connection between astrology and gemology lies in its cultural, spiritual, and personal significance for individuals who believe in their combined effects. Many people turn to gemstones as a form of remedy or as a way to align themselves with positive Cosmic energies.

It's important to note that the connection between astrology and gemology is a matter of belief, and it may not be supported by scientific evidence. While some people find value and positive experiences in wearing gemstones based on astrological guidance, others may not resonate with this approach. The relevance of astrological gemology ultimately depends on an individual's beliefs and their personal experiences with its effects.

ASTROLOGICAL EFFECTS OF PRECIOUS GEMSTONES.

Gemstones have a special significance in Vedic astrology. Gemstones are used from ages of ages to liberate the problems caused by planets. In the days before, only the kings and people with high levels used to wear gemstones recommended by Astrologers and have their benefits, but now a day's anyone can wear and get the benefits of the gemstones.

Wearing gemstones for planetary relieve in today's prevalence is growing rapidly, because the people who are wearing these gems are benefiting from them in every area of life whether it may be progress in business, education, illness etc. Now a days from the Bollywood to industrialist everyone is taking advantage of gemstones.

It is necessary to know about the gemstone, we are going to wear and whether that is going to impart good or bad effects according to our horoscope chart or not, otherwise, in the case of opposition, it can also do harm rather than benefit. So, a note of **CAUTION** –

If we want to wear a Gemstone always do consult an experienced Astrologer before we wear them.

AN ASTRO-GEMOLOGICAL CORELATION OF NATURAL GEMSTONES w.r.t THE NINE PLANETS

Astrological gemology is a belief that certain gemstones are associated with specific planets and can influence a person's astrological attributes and destiny. This practice is deeply rooted in ancient traditions and is often used as a remedy in Vedic astrology. Here is a list of natural gemstones commonly associated with the nine planets in Vedic astrology:

1. **Sun (Surya):** Ruby (Manikya)
   - The ruby is believed to enhance the Sun's positive influence and can promote leadership, confidence, and vitality.

2. **Moon (Chandra):** Pearl (Moti)
   - The pearl is associated with the Moon and is believed to enhance emotional balance, intuition, and calmness.

3. **Mars (Mangal):** Red Coral (Moonga)
   - The red coral is said to strengthen the energy of Mars and can aid in courage, confidence, and physical well-being.

4. **Mercury (Budh):** Emerald (Panna)
   - The emerald is believed to enhance Mercury's attributes, promoting communication skills, intellect, and business acumen.

5. **Jupiter (Guru):** Yellow Sapphire (Pukhraj)
   - The yellow sapphire is associated with Jupiter and is thought to bring wisdom, luck, and spiritual growth.

6. **Venus (Shukra):** Diamond (Heera)
   - The diamond is believed to enhance the qualities of Venus, promoting love, beauty, creativity, and prosperity.
7. **Saturn (Shani):** Blue Sapphire (Neelam)
   - The blue sapphire is associated with Saturn and is believed to bring discipline, focus, and protection from negative energies.
8. **Rahu:** Hessonite Garnet (Gomed)
   - The hessonite garnet is linked to Rahu and is believed to counteract malefic influences, promote focus, and spiritual growth.
9. **Ketu:** Cat's Eye Chrysoberyl (Lehsunia)
   - The cat's eye chrysoberyl is associated with Ketu and is believed to aid in spiritual insight, intuition, and protection.

It's important to note that Astrological gemology is a belief system and is not scientifically proven. While these associations have cultural and traditional significance, their efficacy and impact vary based on individual beliefs. If you are considering using gemstones for astrological purposes, it's advisable to consult with a knowledgeable astrologer or gemologist and make an informed decision based on your personal beliefs and preferences.

Table for Selection of Astrological Gemstones as per One's Rashi (Zodiac Sign)

Rashi	Lord of Rashi	Your Gem	Finger to Wear
1.Aries / Mesha	Mars	Red Coral	Ring finger
2.Taurus /Vrishbha	Venus	Diamond	Ring finger
3.Gemini / Mithun	Mercury	Emerald	Little finger
4. Cancer / Karka	Moon	Pearl	Ring finger
5. Leo / Simha	Sun	Ruby	Ring finger
6. Virgo / Kanya	Mercury	Emerald	Little finger
7. Libra /Tula	Venus	Diamond	Ring finger
8. Scorpio / Vrichika	Mars	Red Coral	Ring finger
9. Sagittarious / Dhanu	Jupiter	Yellow Sapphire	First finger
10. Capricon / Markar	Saturn	Blue Sapphire	Middle finger
11. Aquarius / Kumbh	Saturn	Blue Sapphire	Middle finger
12. Pisces / Meena	Jupiter	Yellow Sapphire	First finger

3

NATURAL GEMS: NORMS, PROCEDURE & USAGE

Proper selection, shape, colour and use of gemstones can transform into therapeutic power tools.

The potent healing energy of therapeutic gems can deeply heal and nourish every aspect of the human form.

The gems' energy goes to work dissolving energetic blockages and producing beneficial changes in the body, mind, and emotions. These Gem stones do work, giving an ample scope for alternate medicine. But one should be very cautious and careful in choosing the right stone and Gem.

Rules to wear gems:
- We should always consult a good astrologer before wearing a gem. Here are the few points which we should always refer before wearing a gem:
- Before wearing a gem, one should check the position of planet, dasha, antardasha of planet, the lordship of houses.
- One can wear a gem for any combust or weak planet to increase the power of that planet.
- We can wear a gem for a retrograde malefic planet.
- Gems are not only a part of fashion but gems have amazing characteristics to provide remedy for certain

diseases also. Generally, in Ayurveda gems are being used to make different bhasm and medicines which helps to recover in different mental and physical diseases.

For maximum benefits of gemstones effect, one must take care of the following points:

- First, correctly diagnose the problem/disorders. Find the planet associated and its reason.
- Find a good gemstone with the correct weight.
- Prana Pratishtha must be done through Vedic mantras.
- Get a ring of the metal prescribed to you by an astrologer or a Gem Specialist.
- Before wearing the ring, energise the stone through the correct process.
- To wear the ring, find the appropriate occasion, the planet's position, and star.
- Neither put the ring on the ground nor let anyone else wear it.

NORMS, PROCEDURE, DAY, TIME AND MANTRA FOR WEARING GEMSTONES

Wearing gemstones for astrological or metaphysical purposes is a practice that involves specific norms, procedures, days, times, and mantras to harness the gemstone's energies for personal betterment. These practices are often associated with Vedic astrology and other belief systems. Here are the general guidelines:

1. **Consultation with an Astrologer or Gemologist:**
   - Before wearing a gemstone, it's crucial to consult with a qualified astrologer or gemologist who can analyse your birth chart (Kundali) and recommend the most suitable gemstone based on your planetary positions and objectives.

2. **Gemstone Selection:**
   - The astrologer will suggest a gemstone that corresponds to a specific planet in your birth chart. Common gemstone-planet associations include:
   - Ruby (Sun), Pearl (Moon), Yellow Sapphire (Jupiter), Emerald (Mercury), Diamond (Venus), Blue Sapphire (Saturn), Coral (Mars), Hessonite Garnet (Rahu), and Cat's Eye (Ketu).
   - The astrologer will also consider the quality, colour, and carat weight of the gemstone.

3. **Gemstone Acquisition:**
   - After selecting the appropriate gemstone, acquire it from a reputable and certified gem dealer to ensure its authenticity and quality.

4. **Gemstone Purification and Activation:**
   - Purification is an essential step before wearing a gemstone. It removes any negative energies or influences associated with the gem.
   - The gemstone is typically soaked in milk, honey, ghee (clarified butter), and water for a prescribed period, followed by a ritual cleansing with sacred water (Ganga jal) or cow's milk.

- The gemstone is then energized or activated through specific mantras and rituals, often performed by a priest or astrologer.

5. **Auspicious Day and Time:**
   - The timing of wearing a gemstone is crucial. It is typically done on an auspicious day and during a specific planetary hour (Hora) that aligns with the associated planet.
   - Some people prefer to wear the gemstone during a planetary transit (Gochara) or on the day of the planet's ruling deity (e.g., Sunday for the Sun).

6. **Right Finger or Hand:**
   - The gemstone is usually worn on a specific finger or hand based on astrological recommendations:
   - **Ring Finger (Fourth Finger):** Common for most gemstones.
   - **Right Hand:** For males.
   - **Left Hand:** For females.

7. **Metal Setting:**
   - The gemstone is often set in a metal ring or pendant. The choice of metal (gold, silver, or others) may also be determined by astrological considerations.

8. **Reciting Mantras:**
   - Mantras associated with the ruling planet of the gemstone are chanted while wearing it. For example, for a ruby (associated with the Sun), the Gayatri mantra or Surya mantra can be recited.

9. **Regular Maintenance:**

    -   Gemstones should be periodically cleansed, re-energized, and checked for any damage or discoloration. This is typically done during specific planetary transits or on the gemstone's birthday (based on the date of acquisition).

10. **Belief and Intent:**

    -   It's important to wear the gemstone with a positive mindset, belief in its potential benefits, and a clear intention for betterment.

Remember that the effectiveness of gemstones is a matter of belief and faith. While many individuals find value in wearing gemstones as astrological remedies or for personal growth, results can vary from person to person. Always seek guidance from a qualified astrologer or Gemmologist for personalized advice and follow the prescribed procedures diligently.

4

GEMS AS PER THE SEVEN DAYS OF THE WEEK

I) RUBY – MANIKYA – SUN – RAVI – SUNDAY

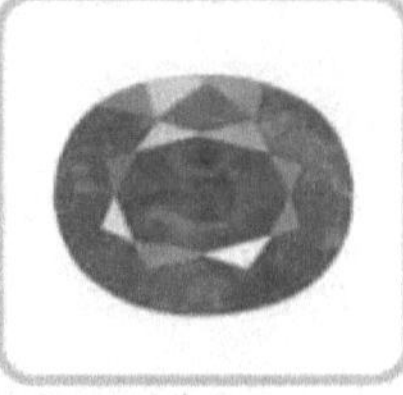

Ruby is the costliest Gemstone worn for Sun, emitting red cosmic rays and infra-red radiation, makes and gives the subject active, smart, bestows high honour and social esteem, freedom from sight problems and eye defects/ailments.

Ruby - Manik

This Gemstone rules over bones, headaches, indigestion, fevers and colic. In short, the wearer will be generally favoured with good health, position and prestige, particularly making him/her free from any serious abnormalities or disease.

Gem therapists, sculptors, artists, engineers, architects, legal experts, high court judges can wear Ruby Gemstone with a great advantage.

II) PEARL – MOTI – MOON – SOM – MONDAY

Pearl is a wide shining Gemstone in several varieties of shell fish.

Pearls coming from Basrah and Gulf countries and Mediterranean region are of pure quality and highly beneficial, particularly in reducing tensions, stomach ailments and marital discards

If this Gemstone is worn by the ladies on neck, it will preserve their chastity.

This Gemstone influence over heart, blood and mind is considerable. It increases the self-confidence of the wearer and enhances his/her mental faculties, promotes and builds cordial working atmosphere around him or her.

III) CORAL – MOONGA – MARS – MANGAL – TUESDAY

Coral is a precious Gemstone of bright red colour and it comes in lighter shades too.

Coral Gemstone flourish at the hollow of the seas.

Red Coral - moonga

An opaque Gemstone is most effective for female or male for powerful emotions through absorption of red radiation from visible light spectrum.

Through use of this gemstone in gold, several diseases can be warded off, particularly tropical fevers, chicken pox, jaundice, fistula, impotency and ailments pertaining to blood. Particularly impure blood.

Its use is also most effective in healing ailments like anaemia, general debility, weakness, lassitude, body pain allergies, inflammations, cough and cold, bronchitis, pneumonia etc.

IV) EMERALD – PANNA – MERCURY – BUDH – WEDNESDAY

Emerald is a precious Gemstone of green colour. It is also known as Panna Gemstone.

Emerald - Panna

It is worn for Mercury and allowed cold green radiation to be absorbed by the wearer enabling him to have perfect control of nervous and intestinal portions, liver, tissues, lunges, vocal cord, tongue and nervous system.

Emerald Gemstone specially recommended for business men, writers, printers, publishers, dealers of scientific instruments.

This Gemstone is also useful for any ailment connected with these functions, defect in recalling, stammering, harshness in voice, students having week IQ and for women in delivery bed fearing complications.

V) YELLOW SAPPHIRE – PUKHRAJ – JUPITER – BRISHAPAT – THURSDAY

Yellow Sapphire Gemstone as its name implies, it is Gemstone of light yellow colour. 

It is an expensive stone and denotes righteousness, piety and truthfulness of the wearers.

Its communed for economic prosperity and comforts and is particularly good for those engaged in business or industry.

Yellow Sapphire Gemstone is particularly good for those desirous to be blessed with children, or those interested in nobler aspects of life and in the occult, charity, spiritual motivation, yoga meditation and religious preaching.

VI) DIAMOND – HEERA – VENUS – SHUKRA – FRIDAY

Diamond is the Gemstone of white colour. Diamond Gemstone is good for all around financial prosperity and happiness. 

By wearing this Gemstone, the wearer will be known for his systematic, methodical and upright approach to the problems of life.

He would also exhibit wisdom and maturity in their dealings, relationship and people would repose confidence in them.

VII) BLUE SAPPHIRE – NEELAM – SATURN – SHANI – SATURDAY

Sapphire has long associations with peace and happiness, and is believed to help with communication, insight, intuition, inspiration and prayer.

The ancients believed that sapphires could help them to predict the future.

5

GEMS: ITS PROPERTIES & CHARACTERISTICS – (TF)

Tabulated formats of the Gemstones represented Daywise with its coressponding Effects interpretating the Characteristics & Properties.

		1	2	3	4	5
SR.	DAYS	GEMS ENG/HIN	NATURAL GEMS IMAGE	SECONDARY CHOICE GEM	GEMS FEATURES	GEMS METAL
1	SUNDAY	MANIK / RUBY	Ruby - Manik	RED SPINAL & RED TOURMALINE	Status, Fame increases, To speak truth	GOLD
2	MONDAY	MOTI / PEARL		MOONSTONE & SEA WATER PEARL	To make decisions, Control alcohol, cough and cold, for no control on emotions	SILVER
3	TUESDAY	MUNGA / RED CORAL	Red Coral - moonga	CARMELLION & BLOODSTONE	Blood related diseases, laziness, sex arousement, Speech improvement	GOLD
4	WEDNESDAY	PANNA / EMERALD	Emerald - Panna	PERIDOT & GREEN TOURMALINE	Intelligence, Health, Business, for Abdomen problem, Job improvement	GOLD

6	7	8	9	10
FINGER TO BE WORN	**ASSOCIATED MANTRA**	**PROPIATION DAY & TIME**	**GEM & ITS EFFECTS**	**GEM & ITS REMEDIES**
SUN / ANAMIKA / RH – RING 3rd FINGER	Aum Grinih Suryaya Namaha Repeat 7 times	SUNDAY – SUNRISE	STIMULATING, VITALIZING	Promotes expansion; enhances vitality; aids circulation in the etheric body; promotes thermal balance
MERCURY / KANISHTA LH – LITTLE / 4th FINGER	Aum Som Saumaya Namaha Repeat 11 times	MONDAY – EVENING	ACTS AS A TONIC, LAXATIVE	Aids understanding; serves as essence of lunar energy.
SUN / ANAMIKA / RH – RING 3rd FINGER	Aum Ang Angarakaya Namaha Repeat 19 times	TUESDAY – 1 HOUR AFTER SUNRISE	GIVES STRENGTH & WILLINGNESS TO MEET CHALLENGES & CRITICAL SITUATIONS.	Overcoming skin related problems; Purifies blood and protects individual against cut, wounds, and injuries.
MERCURY / KANISHTA RH-LITTLE-4th	Aum Bum Budhaya Namaha Repeat 19 times	WEDNESDAY – 2 HOUR AFTER SUNRISE	BALANCING, RELAXING, HEALING	Balances; attunes to the life force; clarifies decision making, increases clairvoyance and clairaudience

SR.	DAYS	1 GEMS ENG/HIN	2 NATURAL GEMS IMAGE	3 SECONDARY CHOICE GEM	4 GEMS FEATURES	5 GEMS METAL
5	THURSDAY	PUKHRAJ / YELLOW SAPPHIRE		YELLOW TOPAZ & YELLOW BERYL	For all good things. Cure for all illnesses	GOLD
6	FRIDAY	HEERA / DIAMOND		WHITE SAPPHIRE & WHITE BERYL	For clear speech problems, Develops Aesthetics sense, Romantic, Attraction, Beauty	SILVER
7	SATURDAY	NEELAM / BLUE SAPPHIRE		LOLITE KYANITE	For everything slowing down (work related)	GOLD

6	7	8	9	10
FINGER TO BE WORN	**ASSOCIATED MANTRA**	**PROPIATION DAY & TIME**	**GEM & ITS EFFECTS**	**GEM & ITS REMEDIES**
JUPITER / TARJANI RH – INDEX 1st FINGER	Aum Brim Brishpataya Namaha Repeat 21 times	THURSDAY – 1 HOUR BEFORE SUNSET	GENTLENESS, WEALTHY, FAITHFULNESS.	Most effective to migraine, for cough cold; liver ailments; nervous disorders; loss of appetite.
MERCURY / KANISHTA RH-LITTLE-4th	Aum Shum Shukraya Namaha Repeat 16 times	FRIDAY – SUNRISE	SEDATING, PROMOTES SELF CONTROL	Intensely stimulates an alignment of personal will with divine will.
SATURN / MADHYAMA RH – MIDDLE / 2nd FINGER	Aum Sham Shanaiscaraya Namaha Repeat 23 times	SATURDAY – 2 HOUR 40 MIN. BEFORE SUNSET	CALMING, PURIFYING	Stimulates transmutation of habit patterns on all levels; increases optimistic outlook.

PALMISTRY

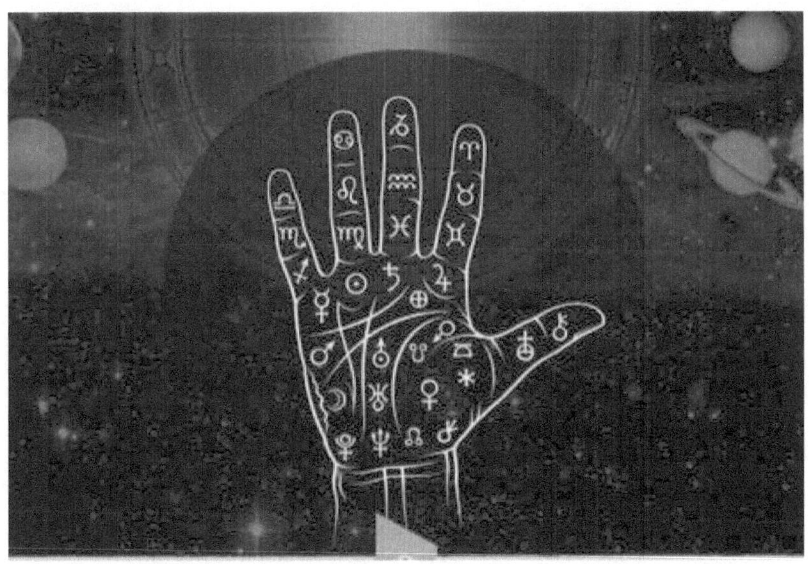

1

INTRODUCTION

Palmistry, also known as **Chiromancy** or palm reading. It is the practice of examining the lines, shapes, and features of a person's hands, specifically the palms, to gain insights into their personality, character, and potential life events. It is a form of divination and has been practiced for centuries in various cultures around the world.

Palm reading interpretation is done preferably by interpreting palms of both the hands simultaneously – its lines, shape and size together.

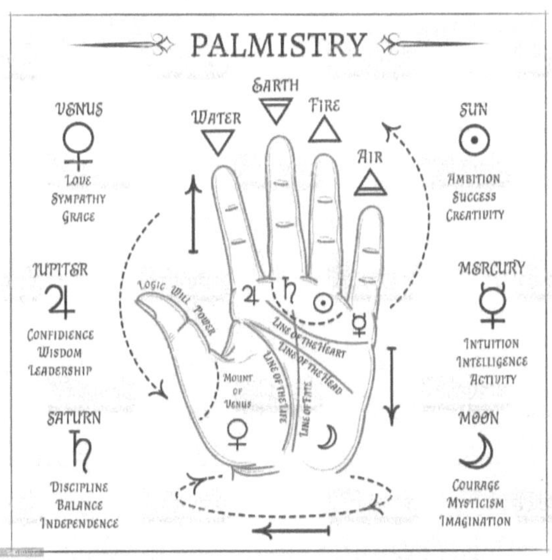

Here's an introduction to the basics of palmistry:

Components of Palmistry: The primary components of palmistry include:

1. **Lines on the Palm:**
    *   **Heart Line:** Located just below the fingers, the heart line is associated with emotions, relationships, and matters of the heart.
    *   **Head Line:** Running horizontally across the palm below the heart line, the head line relates to intellect, decision-making, and thought processes.
    *   **Life Line:** Curving around the base of the thumb, the life line is often linked to one's life path, general well-being, and vitality.
    *   **Fate Line (or Destiny Line):** This line is not present on everyone's palm. It is associated with one's destiny, career path, and significant life events.
    *   **Sun Line (or Apollo Line):** Also, not present on all palms, the sun line is linked to creativity, talent, and fame.
2. **Mounts:**
    *   The mounts are raised areas at the base of each finger and on the palm. They are named after the planets in astrology (e.g., Mount of Venus, Mount of Jupiter) and are associated with specific qualities and characteristics. The condition and prominence of these mounts are considered in palmistry.
3. **Fingers:**
    *   Palmists examine the fingers for their length, shape, and flexibility.

- **Finger Length:** The length of the fingers can indicate various personality traits. Long fingers are often associated with analytical thinking, while short fingers may suggest practicality.
- **Finger Shapes:** The shape of each finger, whether pointed or square-tipped, can provide additional insights into personality and character.
- **Fingernails:** The shape, condition, and markings on the fingernails can offer insights into a person's health and habits.

4. **Palm Shape and Finger Placement:**
   - The overall shape of the palm and the placement of fingers relative to each other are examined for their significance. For example, fingers that are widely spaced may suggest an open and adventurous personality, while close-set fingers may indicate a cautious and reserved nature.

5. **Minor Lines and Markings:**
   - In addition to the major lines, palmists also consider minor lines and markings, such as the marriage lines, children's lines, and intuition lines. These lines and markings provide additional details about a person's life and experiences.

6. **Fingerprints:**
   - The patterns of fingerprints are unique to each individual and can provide insights into their life purpose and potential. Some palmists also study fingerprints for their significance.

7. **Texture and Consistency:**
   - The texture, consistency, and overall condition of the skin on the palm and fingers are examined as they may provide clues about a person's health and lifestyle.

8. **Hands and Finger Flexibility:**
   - The flexibility of the hands and fingers can reveal information about adaptability and ease in handling change.

9. **Hand Shapes:** The overall shape and proportions of the hand, as well as the placement of fingers relative to each other, can convey an additional information. There are four primary hand shapes:
   - **Earth Hands:** Square palms with short fingers; associated with practicality and stability.
   - **Air Hands:** Square or rectangular palms with long fingers; linked to intellectual and communicative traits.
   - **Water Hands:** Long palms with long fingers; associated with intuition and sensitivity.
   - **Fire Hands:** Square or rectangular palms with short fingers; linked to energy, assertiveness, and creativity.

How Palmistry Works: Palmistry involves the following steps:

1. **Examination:** A palmist, or palm reader, carefully examines the lines, shapes, and features of a person's hand.
2. **Interpretation:** Based on the observations, the palmist interprets the significance of the lines, shapes, and

mounts. They consider both individual elements and the overall configuration of the hand.

3. **Analysis:** The palmist analyse the information to provide insights into the person's personality traits, strengths, weaknesses, and potential life path. They may also offer guidance on specific aspects of the person's life, such as relationships and career.

RELEVANCE OF PALMISTRY

Palmistry is often used for self-discovery, personal growth, and self-awareness. Some people consult palmists for relationship compatibility assessments or career guidance. It's important to note that palmistry is considered a pseudoscience, as its claims have not been empirically validated. Interpretations provided by palmists are often based on cultural beliefs, traditions, and intuition rather than scientific evidence. These Interpretations should be taken with an open mind and used as a tool for self-exploration and self-awareness rather than as definitive predictions

1. **Self-Discovery:** Palmistry is often used as a tool for self-discovery and self-awareness. People seek palmistry readings to gain insights into their personality traits, strengths, weaknesses, and life path.

2. **Relationships:** Palmistry can provide insights into one's compatibility with others, making it a popular tool for relationship and marriage compatibility assessments.

3. **Career Guidance:** Some individuals consult palmists for career guidance and insights into their aptitudes and potential career paths.

4. **Personal Development:** Palmistry can be used as a means of personal development and growth. Understanding one's traits and tendencies can help individuals make positive changes in their lives.

THE PRIMARY LINES

A Complete Hand with All Major Indications & Description of the Major Lines on the Palm.

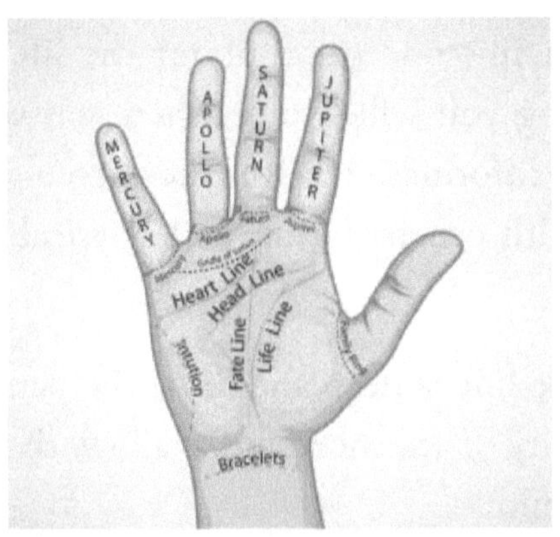

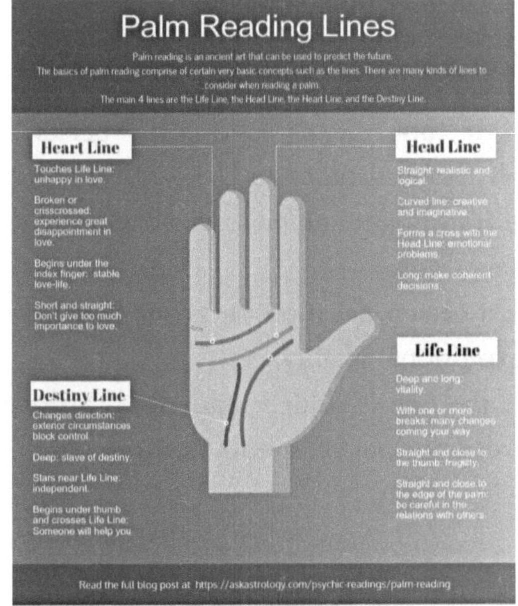

LIFE LINE

The line on the palm that people are most curious about is the life line. This line begins between the index finger and the thumb and continues downward toward the base of the thumb and the connection to the wrist.

A common misconception about the life line is that it reveals how long you will live or when you will die. It does however, reveal information about the encounters in your life, relationships with others, health and physical and emotional well-being.

- If the line is deep and long, the person has a lot of vitality. If it's short and shallow, the person is very credulous.
- If the Life-Line has one or more breaks in it, the person will experience many changes in their life situation.
- If it forms a half-circle, the person has strong physical resistance and a hearty appetite for life.
- If it's straight and close to the thumb, the person is very fragile.
- If a person has more than one Life-Line, they have exceptional vitality.
- If the line is straight and close to the edge of the palm, the person should be careful in their relations with others.

Long and deep line: Indicates good health, stamina, vitality and a well-balanced individual.

Short and deep line: Indicates the ability to overcome physical problems. It is a myth that a short life line signifies a short life. If the life line is short and shallow, it may signify that other people can easily influence or control you.

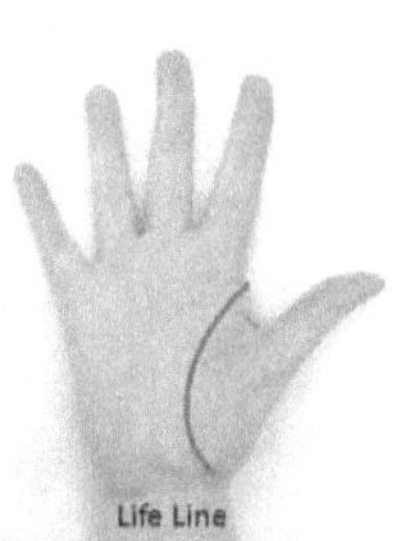

Deep line: Indicates a smoother life path.

Faint line: Indicates a person with low energy and having a less adventurous life.

Broken line: Indicates struggles, losses, unexpected change or interruption in your way of living, an accident or an illness. A break in the life line on one hand can signify that you may get ill and recover quickly. A break in the life line on both hands can signify that you may suffer a serious illness or disease. If there is a break near the wrist area in the line, it can indicate problems in early childhood.

Chained line: You are susceptible to health or emotional problems. You may also experience a life path that takes you in many directions.

Forked line: This type of line has various meanings depending on the fork placement on the hand. Generally, forks indicate an interruption, redirection or life change. It can sometimes mean that you are surrounded by scattered or split energies. If it leads to the Mount of Jupiter, it indicates success and recognition. If it forks to the Mount of Moon, it indicates traveling to far off places.

Double or triple line: Indicates that you are surrounded by positive energies and you have great stamina. You might possibly be a twin or have found a true partner and soul mate, or you have someone watching over you. However, it may also mean that you are living a double life.

Absent line: Indicates a high-strung, anxious and nervous individual.

Branched line: Upward branches indicate achievement and success and downward branches indicate poor physical and emotional health, money problems, feelings of sadness and loss. Lines extending up and above the life line show an ability to recover from situations. Lines extending below the life line signify habitually wasting energy.

HEAD LINE

- The head line, also known as the **wisdom line**, reveals mental and psychological makeup and intellectual development and intuitive abilities.
- This line begins just above the life line, between the thumb and the index finger and runs across the palm toward the other edge of the palm horizontally.
- Sometimes the head line begins directly on the life line and extends out from there. This means that you have a

strong will; mind over matter. Forked lines are sometimes called the writer's fork or the lawyer's fork.

- The Head-Line corresponds to intellectual faculties, creativity, logic, communication, and the acquisition of knowledge.
- When this line is wavy, it means the person has a weak intellect and has trouble concentrating for any length of time.
- When the line is straight, the person is realistic and logical and prefers action to reflection.
- When the line is curved, the person is creative and imaginative. They have original ideas but may be out of touch with reality.
- When a line forms a cross with the Head Line or circles around it, the person will experience emotional problems.
- If the Head-Line is long, the person has a clear vision of things and is very coherent in their decision-making.
- If the Head-Line does not touch the Life Line, the person enjoys travel and gets the most they can out of life.

Long: Indicates intelligence and a good memory. Represents an individual who thinks things through and does not overreact. They look at many possibilities before taking action.

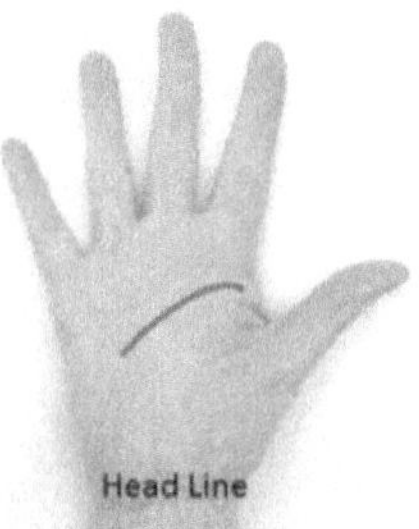

Very long, extending across entire palm: Indicates a very successful individual and not the cowardly type. May have a tendency to be selfish.

Long and straight: Indicates a versatile, complex individual.

Straight: This indicates an individual who is realistic, down-to-earth, unimaginative, materialistic, logical, good organizational skills or a having great attention to detail.

Short: This indicates a practical and non-complex individual and someone who does not beat around the bush.

Deep: This denotes an excellent memory, concentration and a sensible nature.

Wavy: This signifies inner conflict with an individual's practical and emotional sides. It can also indicate an individual who is untrustworthy, restless, unstable or has a short attention span.

Curved or sloping: Indicates a romantic and creative and idealistic individual who is open to new ideas and is not afraid to investigate concepts or beliefs. This person trusts his inklings and intuition.

Faint: This signifies inability to concentrate or a lack of common sense, a daydreamer.

Broken: Indicates inconsistent thinking or nervousness and mental exhaustion.

Crosses: These indicate the vital and crucial decisions made in one's life that can have a direct impact on your fate in your life.

Chained: This signifies an individual who is undergoing personal conflict, melancholy or confusion and can have a problem setting positive goals.

Forked: If the line ends with a strong fork, it is called a writer's fork or lawyer's fork. This person enjoys debate and can see both sides of an issue. This indicates great imagination and someone who uses his psychic powers and writing and speaking abilities throughout life.

Hooked: This indicates a self-centred, untrustworthy individual. If the hook is low in the palm, the individual can be miserly, selfish and cheap.

Branches: These signify events that are yet to come. They can also represent distractions that take an individual off his intellectual path.

Branched upward: Signifies positive outcomes and success in career, academics and creativity. Sometimes indicates having big dreams without being centered.

Branched downward: Signifies signs of struggle, possible depression, sorrow and distress and disappointments in certain points in life.

Absent: Extremely rare, but it can possibly indicate laziness, sluggishness, dullness or even detachment from reality.

Sister or Double: This can indicate increased brainpower. It can also represent a pleasant person or the direct opposite; a cruel person.

HEART LINE

- The heart line, also known as the **love line** or mensal line, gives an indication about a person's emotional state and their emotional and physical relationships with others.

- This line is located above the head line and life line. It starts either under the index finger or middle finger, and extends toward the little finger. Some clues about love and relationships are revealed just by the position of the line on the palm.

- If the heart line begins underneath the index finger, it is an indication that you are satisfied with your love life, or it could mean that you are picky about who you choose to have a relationship with.

- If it begins underneath the middle finger, this can signify a self-centred approach to love, or you are consumed by the need to be loved.

- A line that starts between the middle and index fingers indicates that you are quick to give away your love. If the line crosses the fate line, it can indicate the possibility of a relationship loss.

- This line corresponds to a person's love-life, emotions, cardiovascular health, mood swings, and state-of-mind.

- If it touches the Life-Line it means the person is usually unhappy in love.

- If the Heart-Line is broken or crisscrossed by many smaller lines, the person has known, or will experience, great disappointment in love, and will have a hard time getting over it.

- If the line begins under the index finger, the person should have a stable love-life.
- If it's short and straight, the person doesn't accord much importance to love.
- If it begins under the third/middle finger, the person is easily infatuated.
- If it begins in the middle of the hand, the person is selfish in love and considers partners property rather than people.
- If it's straight and runs parallel to the Head-Line, the person can control their emotions and are not easily influenced in this area.

Long: Indicates a person who is open and has an overall warmth. It can also indicate having a naive belief that there are perfect relationships.

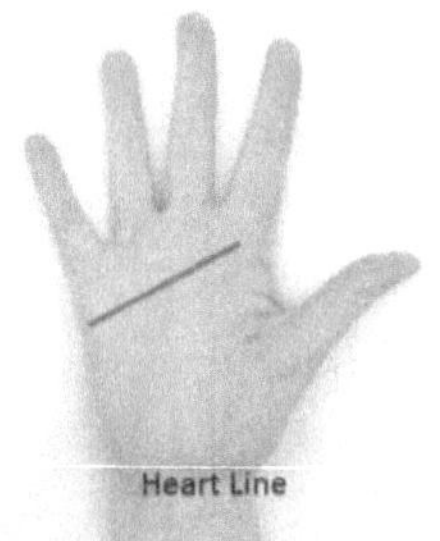

Very long: When the line touches both ends of the palm, it shows signs of co-dependency toward their partners (possible promiscuity).

Short: Indicates a highly self-centered individual, not outgoing.

Deep: Indicates a stressful life.

Deep and straight line: Indicates someone with feelings of jealousy, or having a tendency to disregard authority.

Straight: A more passive person in love relationships, or can signal someone who is void of emotion and or whose emotions are ruled by the brain.

Straight and Short: Indicates an individual not particularly concerned with romance.

Straight and Parallel to the head line: Indicates an emotionally stable individual.

Wavy: Represents many love relationships, or a lack of serious relationships.

Clear and Deep: Indicates sincerity, considerate and respectful, self-secure and at peace with their emotions.

Red and Darker: This type of line represents a temperamental approach to life, which can make you either easy-going or quick-tempered.

Red and Lighter: This type of line represents a more removed, stoic and cold emotional state.

Faint: Represents aloofness and places little importance on emotional life.

Broken: Indicates a person who is often stressed emotionally, can be subject to mood swings, and suffers from emotional trauma.

Chained: Indicates an individual who is easily hurt, has feelings of unhappiness, indecisiveness, or represents a time of depression in your life.

Double Forked: Indicates that your life combines romance with practicality and common sense.

Triple Forked: There is great balancing between your logical, physical and emotional sides.

Curved: Indicates a very physical and emotional, sensitive and intuitive individual. Can represent someone who expresses feelings easily.

Absent: Shows ruthlessness and a person who is ruled by logic and may have a disregard for others.

Without Branches: Indicates a lack in the ability of emotional growth.

Branched upward: Represents a strong interest in the opposite sex and has good and positive relationships.

Branched downward: Represents poor quality or unhappiness in relationships, subject to heartbreak.

FATE OR DESTINY LINE

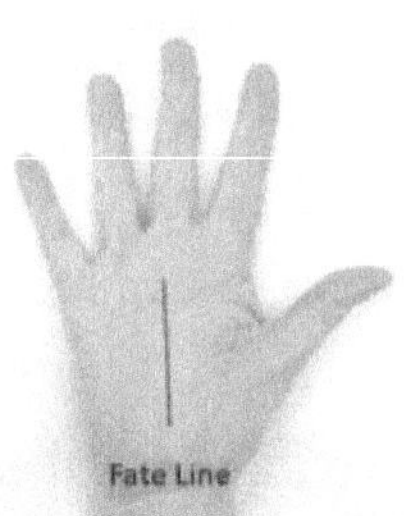

- The Fate Line is also known as the **Line of Destiny**. This line reveals the effects that people and events have had on an individual. These are events that the person has had no control over.
- This line is tied to one's life path. It is also an indication of obstacles that may be faced, educational and occupational choices, accomplishments, achievements and how content an individual is with his life.
- The line also can indicate that elderly family members might be very controlling and one's own needs and wishes are being neglected.

- This line also denotes a personality that can be strong, however, it may indicate struggles that may get in the way of success.
- If there are breaks in the line, hard luck, loss or failure in life can happen. There might be a double or sister line and this signifies a very successful and prominent career, even a renowned one.

This is also sometimes called the **Luck Line**, and indicates a person's degree of autonomy, and how well they control their life.

If the line has breaks inside or changes direction, the person is the victim of exterior circumstances and is not in control of their life.

A deep Destiny-Line indicates a person who is a slave of their own Destiny.

A Destiny-Line that starts near, or approaches the Life Line, indicates someone independent and self-taught.

A Destiny-Line that begins under the thumb and crosses the Life Line means the person will receive help.

If the Destiny Line joins the Life Line in the middle, the person should abandon their interests and become involved in working for the common good, with other individuals who want to evolve and experience happiness.

Here's a little information on fate lines:

- If it is deep and straight, you have a very solid, promising career.
- If it's faint, you don't like your job very much.

- If it has lots of forks coming off it, you've had a very turbulent career.
- If it starts from your life line but later splits off, you've been ambitious since a young age, and prefer an entrepreneurial approach to life.
- If it joins with the life line in the middle, you may have or will later give up your interests and desires for the sake of others.
- If the fate line starts at the base of the thumb and then crosses the life line, your family and friends greatly support you.

3

THE SECONDARY LINES

In palmistry minor lines, or secondary lines, can reveal an individual's talents, interests, strengths and weaknesses. Their meanings can vary, depending on the hand shape, markings, mounts and the other lines nearby or crossing over them.

Minor lines can be very faint or may not even be apparent, which is fairly common. If they do appear on the palm, they will give the palm reader a lot more insight into the subject.

Listed below are nine of the more common minor lines and their general meanings; apollo (sun) line, bracelet (rascette) lines, relationship (marriage) lines, health line, girdle of venus and intuition line etc.

I) APOLLO (SUN) LINE

The Apollo Line, also known as the Line of the Sun, when present, is an indication of success in one's life. This line can indicate creative, self-confident individuals who are extremely capable of following through on a plan of action. They can communicate their ideas well and are sensitive, which makes them primed for success and good fortune.

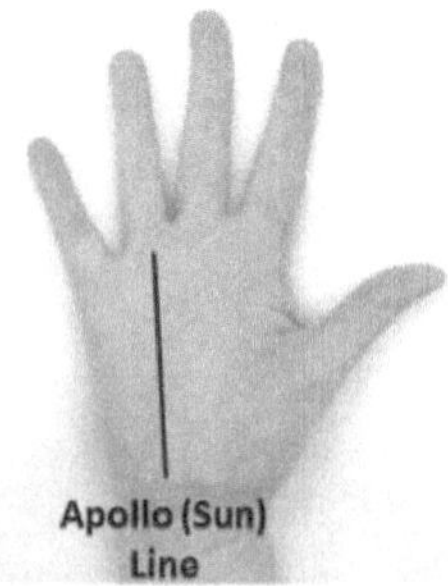

However, the line may not be continuous, due to the fact that life is not free of difficulties.? This may be a sign of inconsistencies in one's life. If this line does not appear on the palm, it does not have any correlation to one's success or failure. Markings on this line can indicate times of illness or setbacks.

II) BRACELET (RASCETTE) LINES

In palmistry, the bracelet lines or rascette lines are considered part of the minor lines. The bracelet/rascette lines are located at the base of the palm on the wrists. The majority of people have three bracelet lines; however, some lucky people have four.

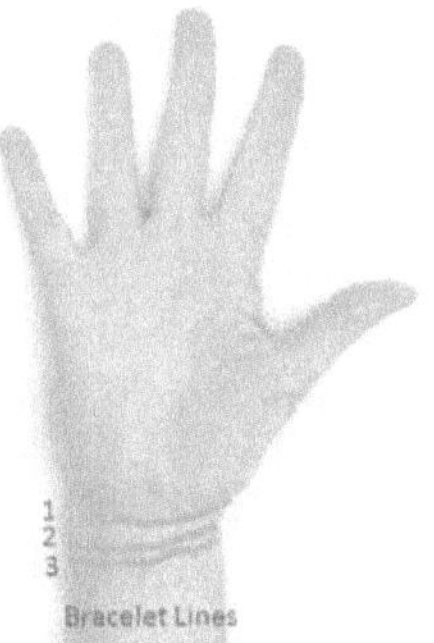

Four lines is an indication that one may live to be close to 100. The lines can reveal a person's longevity, health, destiny, prosperity and the balance or imbalance of the mind, body and spirit. The more solid and unbroken the lines, the better the chances are for a good healthy life.

If the first bracelet line (located closest to the palm) is clear and well defined, without any gaps, breaks or chains, it indicates good health. If it is broken and contains gaps, breaks or chains, it is a sign of overindulgence and not taking responsibility for the proper care of one's health.

If a woman's line is bowed and turned upward, she will come across many obstacles in her life and endure much pain. There may be childbirth complications or she may only have one or two children. If the second line on the wrist bows upward as the first one does, she may endure pain longer than she expected.

If the first bracelet line is chained and the other lines are clear and defined, this may indicate a life of hard work and difficulty in the earlier years, but hopefully, later in life you will have good fortune.

The second bracelet line, if clear and defined, without any gaps breaks or chains, may indicate financial prosperity and a life you can take joy.

The third bracelet line, if clear and defined, without any gaps breaks or chains, can indicate that you can become influential in the community and a well-known individual amongst your peers.

Note, that if you have only one bracelet line, there is a grave possibility that you may not experience the best health during a period in your lifetime or you may experience bouts of depression.

If the first line has a tendency to curve and the next lines are well defined and solid, this is a sign that obstacles were overcome in the early years of life through great effort and hard work to take a healthier path.

If your upper bracelet/rascette lines are chained, it is not always a bad sign. Through all the turmoil that life can bring, having these lines suggest that happiness is not out of reach.

III) CHILDREN LINES

Children lines vertically cross the relationship or marriage lines. They are often very faint. Each line can indicate a child or a potential one. The lines can also reflect an individual who might care for children throughout life, e.g., as a teacher, a counsellor or even as a foster or step parent.

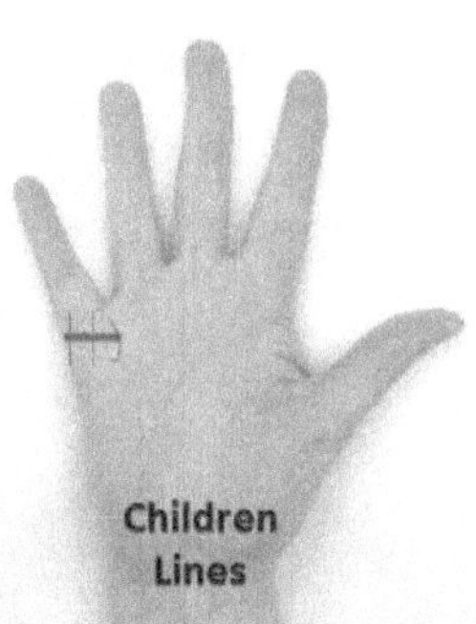

Some palm readers interpret broader children's lines to indicate males and narrower lines to indicate females. Also, clear lines indicate a healthy child; longer lines than the others indicate a child who is a favourite of the parents; uneven or barely visible lines indicate a sensitive child and if that line begins with an island, it represents a child who will have ill health in the early years.

When a child line does not cross the relationship line, it could indicate that a child may come into a relationship later on.

Some palmists say that to find out the number of children you will have, count the vertical lines from the outside of the palm toward the inside.

IV) GIRDLE OF VENUS

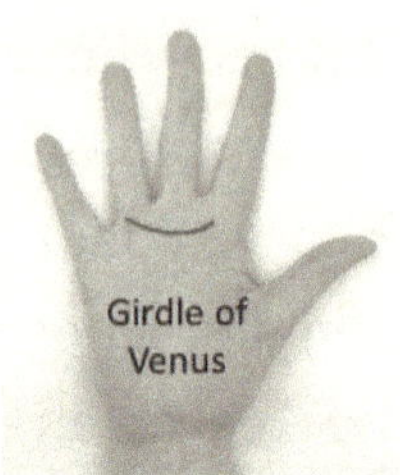

The girdle of Venus can indicate a wound-up and nervous person. These individuals can experience extreme highs and extreme lows. People with this line also may crave excitement and be highly sensual in nature.

If the line has breaks it can represent an individual who needs to keep his temper in check or can indicate a person with deep sensitivities.

V) HEALTH LINE

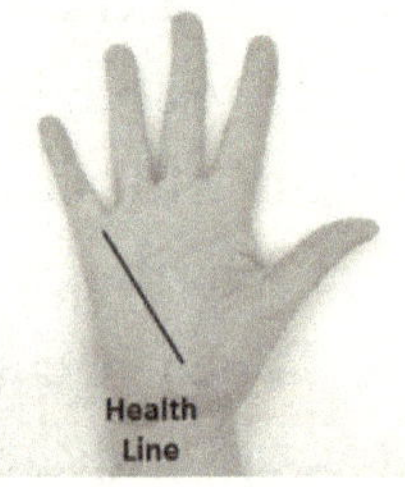

The Line of Health is also known as the Line of Liver, and is an indication of one's health and overall well-being. It can indicate the health of the nervous system, liver and kidneys.

People who have the ability to heal others physically, emotionally or spiritually may possess this line. Keep in mind that if the line appears broken or frayed, it can be an indication of possible illness or those illnesses that have come and gone. Also, it may denote illnesses in partners who are close to you.

VI) INTUITION LINE

The intuition line on the palm signifies individuals who are able to read other people and situations instantly. They are highly intuitive. This line is often very apparent on psychics and psychic mediums. Due to their sensitivity, these individuals may have difficulty in a crowd, as they are sensitive to other people's positive or negative energies.

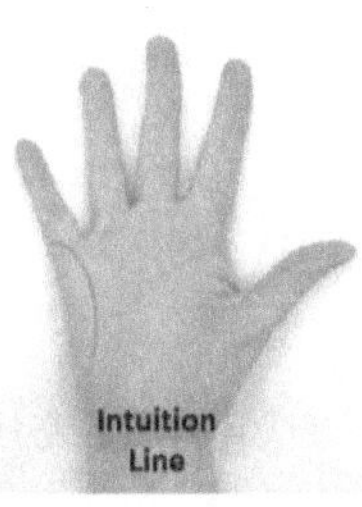

If the intuition line is broken, it may indicate that the individual is overly empathetic and should be careful of their health. If the line is not well pronounced or absent, it does not mean that the individual is not intuitive or even psychic. He may have a psychic hand shape, which is another indicator of psychic abilities.

VII) RELATIONSHIP LINE

The Relationship Lines, also known as Marriage or Love lines, may be one or several, and do not only indicate marriages or partners, but relationships that are significant in one's life. It indicates one's ability to handle relationship commitments.

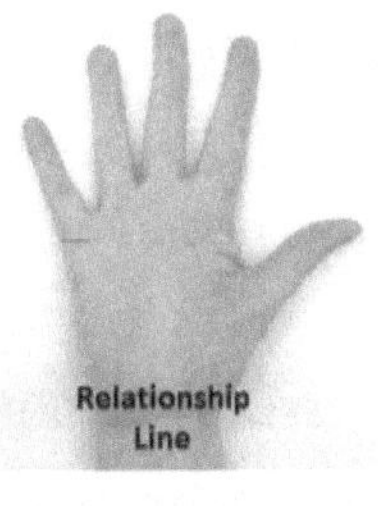

If the lines are well defined and longer, that can indicate a person has the ability to make long-term commitments. Shorter and weaker lines can signify relationships that may not last or ones that may end for a time and begin again. A fork at the end of the lines might signify a divorce.

VIII) RING OF SOLOMON (JUPITER)

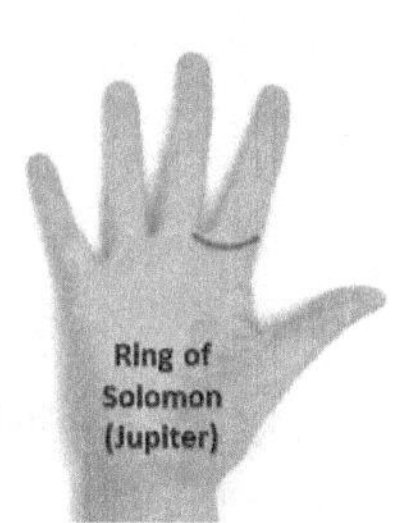

The Ring of Solomon, also referred to as the Ring of Jupiter, is located at the bottom of the Jupiter finger (index finger) on its mount. This ring can appear in a semicircle formation or in a straight line. It represents King Solomon from the Bible and Jupiter, the king of the gods during Roman times.

People who possess this ring have strong leadership qualities and are usually found in positions of authority. They are well respected, intelligent and philosophical individuals who are extremely tolerant and thoughtful of others.

IX) RING OF SATURN

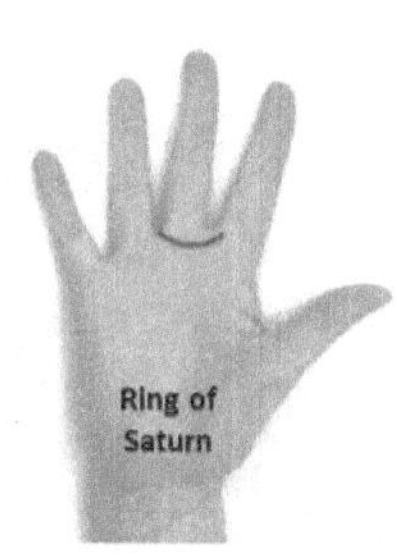

The Ring of Saturn is a semicircle-shaped line located at the base of the middle finger. This ring is not commonly found. The Ring of Saturn may indicate an individual who is unhappy, a hermit, overly serious in nature and not living life to the fullest.

This person may be consumed with a pessimistic outlook on life. You may refer to this person as always being down the dumps.

X) RING OF APOLLO

The Ring of Apollo, which is a very rare marking, signifies that a blockage exists in creativity. This marking might actually block the positive effects of the traits associated with the Apollo finger. If you have this marking, do not be discouraged. Some palmists believe that with a change to a positive outlook, focusing on creative projects and broadening your horizons, this line can dissipate.

4

THE MOUNTS & MARKINGS

In Palmistry, the mounts, or bumps of flesh, on the palm play a very important role during a reading. They are related to the influences of the planets, which also tell us a lot about our physical and emotional makeup.

There are seven mounts on the palms, and they are synonymous with the Sun, Moon, Mars, Mercury, Jupiter, Venus and Saturn. There is also a relationship to the other major and minor lines in the hand, for example, where the mounts may intersect with those lines.

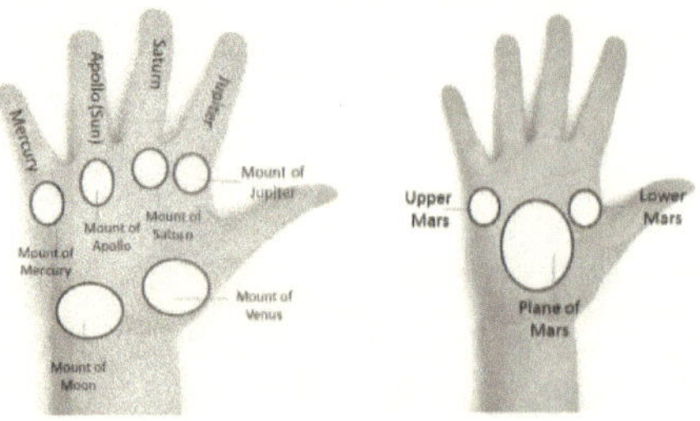

I) MOUNT OF VENUS

The Mount of Venus is located on the palm of the hand at its base, between the thumb and the Life Line. It is an indicator of love, romance, passion, sensuality, the lovers one chooses and physical appearance.

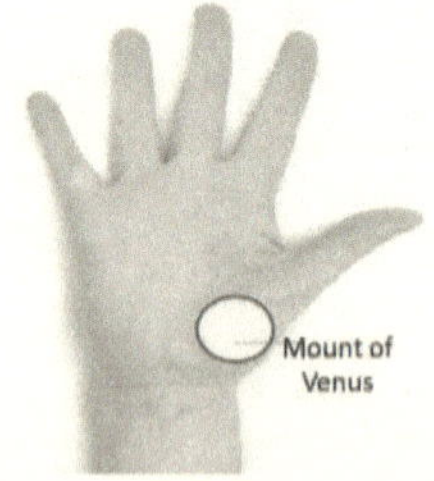

If this mount is normally elevated, it can indicate an attractive and healthy individual who is passionate about the arts and the finer things in life. It can also represent someone who is well respected, influential and enjoys the benefits of true friendships.

If it appears over developed, this may indicate an individual who overindulges and is promiscuous. It can also denote an individual who seeks instant gratification.

A flat or absent Mount of Venus can indicate a person who does not have a connection to family life, faces many troubles and might possibly suffer from an illness or other hardship. It can also indicate someone who easily criticizes others and who is not taken in by physical beauty.

II) MOUNT OF JUPITER

The Mount of Jupiter is located on the palm of the hand at the base of the index finger. It has a connection to the Greek God, Zeus, who became Jupiter in Roman mythology.

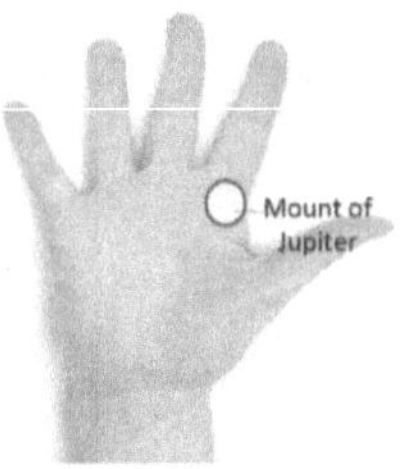

This mount indicates how you perceive the world and how you want to be viewed by others. It has a lot to do with your determination, ego, need for power and control, accomplishment and leadership.

If this mount is normally elevated and prominent, this can indicate an individual who has divine aspects, a strong spiritual connection, is not self-centred and has no problem helping others. This person always has a pleasant look, and no matter how difficult the situation, he carries a positive attitude. He shows signs of good health and respect and compassion for others.

If it appears over developed and higher than the others, this may indicate someone who wants to dominate other people, is self-centred and has a lack of compassion. If there seems to be a flat or absence of this mount, this is an indication that one's self-confidence is low and there is a presence of a lack of ambition.

III) MOUNT OF SATURN

The Mount of Saturn is located on the palm of the hand below the base of the middle finger. It is an indicator of patience, duty and responsibility, as well as one of modesty and a need for solitude.

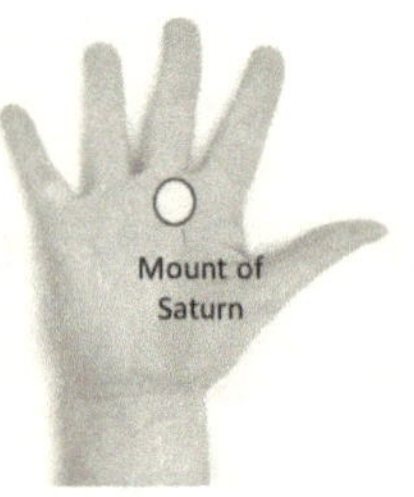

If this mount is normally elevated, it can indicate an individual who is friendly and independent, and one who believes that things happen as they should.

If it appears overly developed, this can mean an individual who is stubborn to a fault, at times depressed, cynical, mistrusting, too shy and too isolated from others.

A flat or absent Mount of Saturn can indicate disorganization, superficiality, and a lack of self-reflection.

IV) MOUNT OF APOLLO (SUN)

The Mount of Apollo, also known as the Mount of the Sun, is located at the base of the ring finger and lies on the upper part of the Heart Line. It indicates one's self-assurance, compassion and stateliness. It indicates a desire to stand out from others in a crowd.

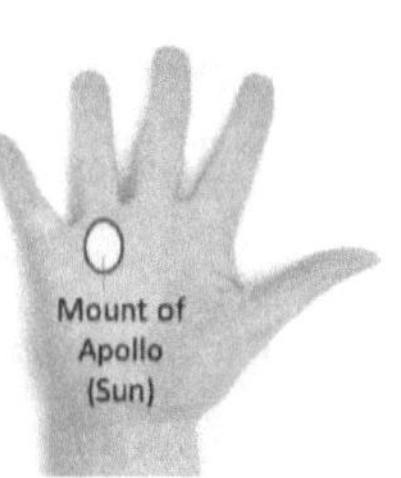

If this mount is normally elevated, it can indicate an outgoing person and someone who is flexible to changes.

When the Mount of Apollo is over-developed, this is an indication of envy, lack of control over one's temper and always causing problems with friends, partners and relationships.

If it is flat or unpronounced, it can indicate a person who is dull and not very outgoing. Making good decisions becomes difficult for this person.

V) MOUNT OF MERCURY

The Mount of Mercury is located on the palm of the hand below the base of the little finger. It is an indicator of business success, finances, practicality, shrewdness, verbal sharpness and adaptability.

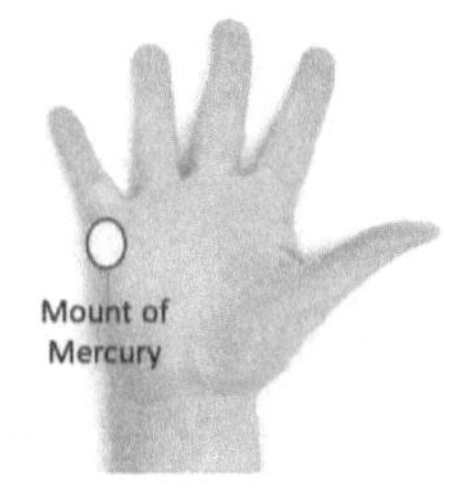

If this mount is well defined, this can indicate an individual who has many interests, is flexible and has very good communication skills. This person will be successful in business or perhaps psychology and is someone who can read people extremely well.

If it appears overly developed, this can signify someone who tends to talk too much and might not always be truthful. The individual can be greedy and overly concerned with the acquisition of money and material goods.

A flat or absent Mount of Mercury can indicate a shy individual who has trouble communicating with others and also someone who will not achieve much financial success in life.

VI) MOUNT OF MOON (LUNA)

The Mount of Moon, also known as the Mount of Luna, is located on the palm of the hand at its base, on the little finger side of the hand. It is an indicator of intuition, creativity and vivid imagination.

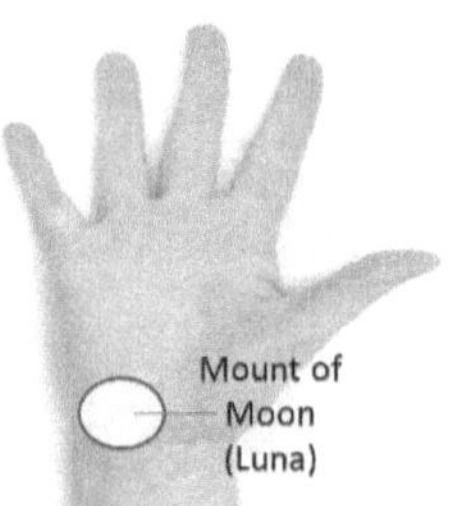

If this mount is well defined, this can indicate a person with excellent creative power. This individual has a love of the arts and nature. It also represents one who has great intuition or psychic abilities, is compassionate and helps any friends in need.

This individual loves the ocean. If it appears overly developed, this individual may be letting his imagination run wild, thus clouding reality. This individual draws himself into his own fantasies.

A flat or absent Mount of Moon can indicate a person who prefers to be at home and one who might have a good imagination, but shares it only with himself. It can also indicate someone devoid of imagination who exhibits pessimism and lacks enthusiasm. This may be a closed down individual, who is deep in his own thoughts.

VII) MOUNTS OF MARS

The Mounts of Mars are located in three areas of the palm. They are an indication of one's ability to deal with confrontation and have been equated to the fight or flight instinct.

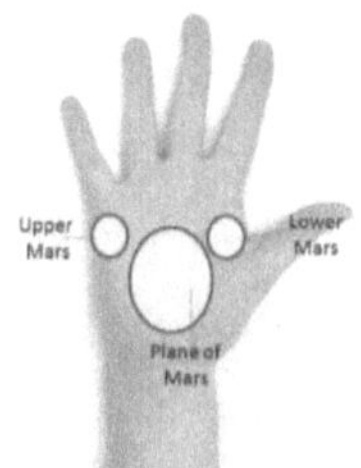

There are many similarities between the Upper and Lower Mounts of Mars; some that are positive and some that are negative. Some palm readers only address the Upper and Lower mounts; however, others include the Plane of Mars in their readings.

The Upper Mount of Mars, or Positive Mars, is positioned between the Head Line and the Heart Line, below the little finger. It reflects temperament.

An overly developed mount denotes a stubborn, defiant individual who is not one to enter into a give and take situation.

If this mount is absent or flat, this is a sign of one's inability to express true feelings. There is an inability to avoid confrontation and anxiety provoking environments.

If it is normally elevated, the individual has strength and is courageous, well balanced and healthy.

The Lower Mount of Mars, or Negative Mars, signifies an individual's enthusiasm or aggression.

If it appears overly developed, this individual may be quick tempered, over indulgent, egotistical and argumentative.

When it appears under developed, absent or flat, it can indicate that a cloud of uncertainty surrounds the individual.

There is also a lack of self-esteem and getting motivated is difficult. This is also a sign of one's inability to express true feelings and having a tendency to withdraw when uncertainty is there.

The Plane of Mars, which is located in the centre of the palm, is also known as the Middle Mars Plane. An undefined Plane of Mars shows a highly self-centred person. This person can also display temper tantrums.

A thick, well-developed, and firm Mars plane indicates a highly energized person and a sociable individual. However, there can be a negative side to this, it may also be an indication of a rebellious individual who has no regard for the law or others.

If the Plane of Mars has a dip in it, the person has a calm and patient temperament.

5

HANDS & FINGERS SHAPES

HANDS & FINGER SHAPES – IMAGES WITH DESCRIPTION

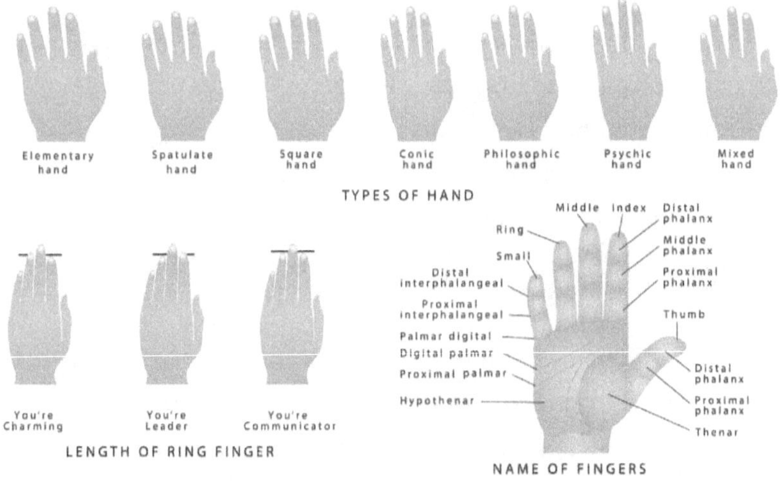

The division of palmistry that deals with the study of the shape of the hand and fingers is known as **Chirognomy.**

Along with the lines, mounts, markings, hand colour, skin texture and flexibility, the shape of the fingers and hands give clues as to what type of characteristics an individual may have.

Six of the basic hand shapes studied in palmistry are **conic, spatulate, pointed or psychic, square, intellectual or**

knotted and mixed. However, there is not only one system used to categorize the hand shapes.

Another method used assigns each hand shape the characteristics of a natural element: earth, air, fire, water, wood and metal. In Western palmistry, the four-element classification is the most common: earth, air, water and fire.

I) HANDS SHAPES & THEIR TYPES

A) SPATULATE HAND

A spatulate hand resembles a spatula, and the fingers and hand are flattened and the fingertips are shaped like a spatula. It is very wide at its base and becomes elongated up toward the fingers.

Individuals having this shape of hand have a good imagination. They constantly search for something to keep them occupied. Their energy is boundless and they are not at all boring.

Most of the time they have a desire for newfound knowledge. Other traits that may be exhibited are impatience, and someone who is unsettled or quick to excite.

B) SQUARE HAND

The square hand has a square-shaped palm, a square wrist, with square or boxy fingertips. One of the most outstanding characteristics is a larger thumb. These hands represent persistent and determined individuals.

They are not ones who do well in chaos, they seek order and conformity with the laws. These individuals are meticulous in their work and are very punctual.

They are people who can be trusted and have no difficulty being honest. They are not confrontational. They are practical and do not usually rely on pure instinct.

C) CONIC HAND

The conic or conical hand tends to have smooth fingers and tapered nails. The palms on a conic hand are broader than the fingers and the width of the hand tapers in toward the fingertips.

Individuals with this type of hand are usually artistic or impulsive in nature. They are individuals who tend toward the physical pleasures in life rather than the intellectual side.

These individuals are easily be influenced by others. They also are experts in the field of the arts and possess great communicative skills. An individual with this shape of hand can sometimes be irresponsible and have a short-fused temper.

D) PHILOSOPHIC (INTELLECTUAL) HAND

The intellectual hand, also known as the knotted hand, is a long-pointed hand with knotty and bony features on the fingers, with large palms that are also bony.

The nails may sometimes appear both square or conical. These hands usually belong to scholarly individuals who choose to use rational thinking. These people learn quickly and are interested in new and creative ideas.

E) PSYCHIC (POINTED) HAND

A pointed hand is also known as a psychic hand. It tends to be a small and slender one, with fingers that are smooth, with long and narrow fingertips. This hand is quite similar to the conical hand.

The palm is medium sized and the thumb appears to be much smaller than the other fingers, however graceful.

People with this type of hand are true visionaries and have an idealistic and dreamy nature. They are interested in divinations and the occult and may be quite psychic. However, they also have an affinity for religion and its rituals and traditions.

On the other hand, they may be lackadaisical in business matters. Punctuality seems to be of little importance to them and they may also lack self-discipline.

F) MIXED HAND

The mixed hand is a combination of 2 or more of the different palmistry hand types – square, conic, pointed, spatulate, or intellectual. These individuals are friendly, flexible and versatile.

II) FINGERS

The fingers are important indicators in palmistry. Each of them reveals a different portion of an individual's character, emotional state, spirituality and health.

They can give insights into an individual's knowledge, intellect, ambition, balance, creativity and communication with others. Their analyses can also help predict one's future or future outcomes.

Palmists consider their shape, length, width, placement, flexibility, horizontal or vertical lines, markings, nail shape etc. Each finger is divided into three sections, called phalanges.

The fingers also contain vertical and horizontal lines. Horizontal lines reveal one's life obstacles and difficulties in the past, present and future. Vertical lines pertain to health issues.

They may also indicate suffering from a lack of sleep. Given below are the general traits for each of the fingers.

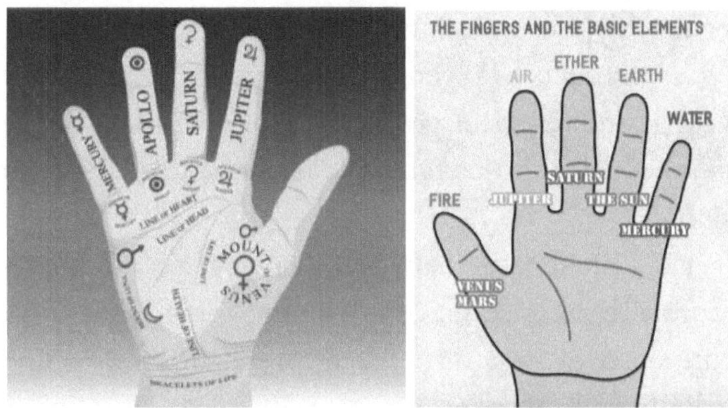

The Astrological Connection of the Fingers

JUPITER FINGER

Jupiter Finger – (Index): This finger influences one's ability to lead. It rules the ego, success and spirituality.

When this finger is long, the individual is strong, set in their ways, likes to take charge and are self-assured. Taken to the extreme, these individuals may stop at nothing to attain their goals.

When the finger is short, the person is shy, full of self-doubt and afraid of failure. Horizontal lines are an indication that someone is going to betray a confidence.

Vertical lines have a direct connection to the health of the thyroid.

SATURN FINGER

Saturn Finger – (Middle): This finger denotes one's ambitions, logic, family and balance.

When the finger is long, it is a sign of someone who is studious and serious about obtaining goals. This is also someone who pays attention to details.

A shorter Saturn finger is an indication of an individual who is not interested in getting ahead or working too hard. This individual is also not afraid to take risks and to make rash decisions.

If it is a bit shorter than the other fingers, intuition plays a great role in decision-making. The horizontal lines represent insecurities with regard to personal relationships and the home life.

Vertical lines deal directly with the health of the pineal gland.

APOLLO FINGER

Apollo/Sun Finger – (Ring): This is the finger that represents creativity, talents, good fortune and success. It indicates personal development and an expansion of one's horizons. This individual is creative and has a deep affection for the arts. The romantic side of one's life is seen through this finger.

An extremely long finger can signify a risk taker and even someone who might have a gambling problem.

When the Apollo finger is short, selfishness and a lack of enthusiasm are present.

When it is even with or leaning toward the Saturn finger, this is an indication of an individual who is self-assured and has a great outlook on life.

The horizontal lines represent a threat to your personal happiness. Vertical lines have an impact on the thyroid or can indicate heart problems.

There is a special marking at the base of this finger that may or may not be present. It is called the ring of Apollo.

MERCURY FINGER

Mercury Finger (Little): This represents communication, intuition and the relationships one has with others.

If this finger is long, the person has a high intelligence level, is a good communicator and is extremely outgoing.

If it is short, one might display childish behaviour, bashfulness and have a lack of self-confidence. This person may also be overly self-critical. Also, if it is bent or twisted, it reveals someone who can be manipulative.

Horizontal lines represent difficulties with self-confidence. It may also suggest a low sex drive.

Vertical lines deal with one's overall health. If it is in line with the other fingers, this is an indication of an individual with good self-esteem and confidence.

6

HAND SHAPES IN CORELATION WITH THE FOUR ELEMENTS OF NATURE

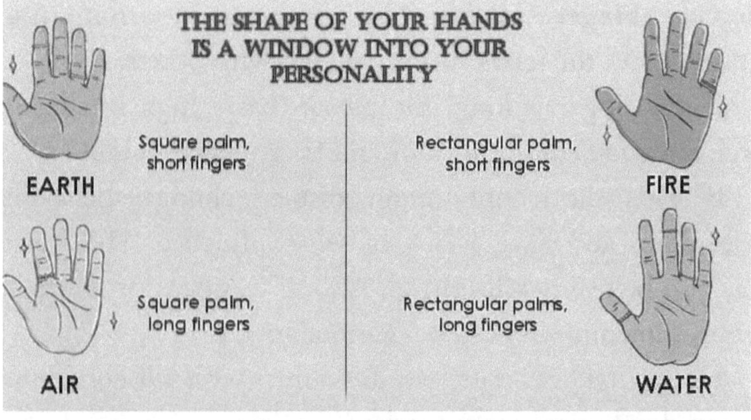

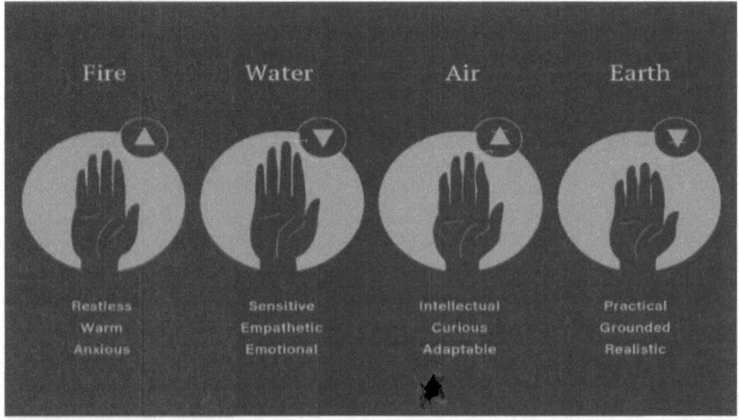

SHAPE OF OUR HANDS DIPCTING OUR PERSONALITY TRAITS w.r.t FOUR ELEMENTS OF NATURE

The simplest type of hand shape classification using the natural elements consists of four elements: earth, air, water and fire. These elements are also used in classifying Astrological signs. But just because you are born under a water sign, e.g., Pisces, it does not mean that your hand will be a water hand.

EARTH HAND: The palm is square, with short fingers. Most people with this hand are practical, hard-working, hands-on and like to be outdoors experiencing nature. They have a realistic approach to life and are dependable and stable in relationships. They can be quick-tempered, stubborn and sometimes display a lack of patience. **This hand shape corresponds to the Astrological signs of Taurus, Virgo and Capricorn**.

AIR HAND: The palm is square, with long fingers. Most people with this hand are mentally active, restless and easily bored. They long for mental challenges, want to expand their knowledge and like to analyse details. They are logical in thought and are excellent communicators. However, sometimes they can worry too much. They do possess good intuitive capabilities and have a tendency to show interest in the psychic realm. **This hand shape corresponds to the Astrological signs of Gemini, Libra and Aquarius.**

WATER HAND: The palm is rectangular and long, with long fingers. Most people with this hand are motivated by their feelings and emotions. Sometimes, in the extreme, they allow their feelings to dictate their lives. They are sensitive in nature and quite creative, especially in the many forms of the arts. They are most content in a calm environment, because they have problems coping with stress. **This hand shape corresponds to the Astrological signs of Cancer, Scorpio and Pisces.**

FIRE HAND: The palm is long and rectangular and the fingers short by comparison. Most people with this hand are outgoing, persuasive and have a tendency to always be the life of the party. They excel when on the go and thrive on it, but do not realize that this can cause burnout and incomplete undertakings. They are usually fun to be around; however, they can turn on a dime. They also can be extremely impatient. **This hand shape corresponds to the Astrological signs of Aries, Leo and Sagittarius.**

7

PALMISTRY & ITS ASTROLOGICAL CONNECTION

The Different Mounts & Its Corresponding Zones Located in the Palm

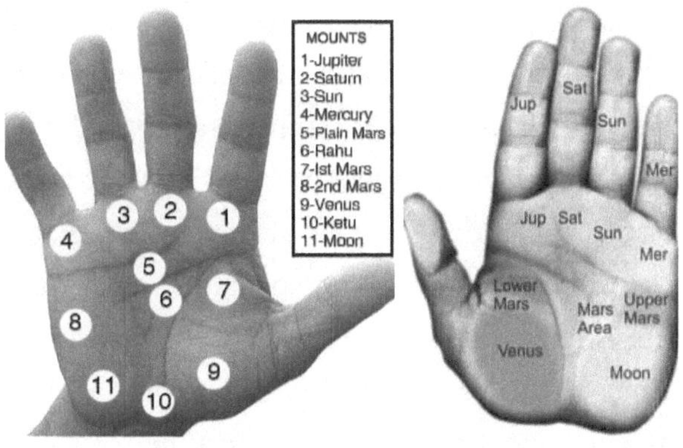

- The planets are associated with the fingers and discrete areas of the palm. These areas are the mounts and zones. The planetary meaning of these features is similar to their use in astrology although there is a different emphasis in meaning. For example, in palmistry the Jupiter finger and the mount beneath it are associated with pride, ambition and high ideals.

- The Saturn finger and the zone beneath it are associated with ethics and morals. Saturn in palmistry is also associated with seriousness, depression and material reality.

- The principles represented by Venus are very similar to those used in Western Astrology, with special emphasis on beauty, art, creativity and self-expression.

- In palmistry Mercury is associated with communication, business and sales acumen, speech and is also associated with relationships. Below the Mercury finger is the beginning of the Heart Line which represents the expression of feelings to other people.

- In palmistry the Moon has a special association with imagination, and in the lowest part of the palm, with psychic energy. It is also associated with travel and movement. In ancient Western Astrology the Moon was also associated with travel because it is the fastest planet and often links the energies of other planets together.

- In palmistry the Sun has a special association with life-giving energy which is expressed in the Life Line. The depth of the solar mount and the quality of the Life Line show the capacity for physical life, general vitality, vim and vigour and enthusiasm. Branches from the Life Line show where enthusiasm is directed.

CONNECTION BETWEEN PALMISTRY AND ASTROLOGY AND ITS RELEVANCE

Palmistry and astrology are both ancient divination practices that offer insights into a person's character, traits, and potential life events. While they are distinct practices, they are often considered complementary due to their shared focus on providing guidance based on individual characteristics and planetary influences. Here's an overview of their connection and relevance:

1. **Interpretation of Personality and Destiny:**
   - **Astrology:** Astrology examines the positions and movements of celestial bodies to interpret how they influence a person's personality, behaviour, and life events. Birth charts are used to analyse planetary positions at the time of a person's birth.
   - **Palmistry:** Palmistry, also known as chiromancy, involves analysing the lines, shapes, and features of a person's hands to interpret their personality traits, inclinations, and potential life paths.
2. **Common Themes:** Both practices share common themes such as personality traits, career inclinations, relationships, health tendencies, and potential life events. They aim to provide insight into an individual's strengths, challenges, and opportunities.
3. **Complementary Insights:** Some practitioners of both palmistry and astrology believe that combining insights from both practices can provide a more holistic understanding of an individual. For example, an astrologer might consider the planetary influences in a person's birth chart alongside palmistry interpretations to offer a comprehensive reading.
4. **Cultural and Spiritual Significance:** Both practices have cultural and spiritual significance in various

societies around the world. They are often used as tools for self-discovery, guidance, and understanding the deeper aspects of life.

5. **Personal Growth and Self-Awareness:** Both palmistry and astrology can serve as tools for personal growth and self-awareness. By gaining insights into one's strengths and challenges, individuals may be better equipped to make informed decisions and navigate their life paths.

Relevance: The relevance of the connection between palmistry and astrology lies in their potential to offer guidance, insight, and self-awareness to individuals seeking to understand themselves better or make important life decisions. People who resonate with the principles of these practices may find them valuable tools for introspection, understanding their life journey, and making informed choices.

It's important to note that both palmistry and astrology are considered divination practices and are not universally accepted as scientifically proven methods. Their relevance is largely subjective, and individuals may choose to engage with them based on their beliefs, cultural background, and personal experiences. As with any form of guidance or self-discovery, it's advisable to approach these practices with an open mind and a discerning perspective.

NUMEROLOGY

1

INTRODUCTION

Numerology is an age-old science that focuses on finding the essence of every personality. It is said to indicate the purpose of your life and the challenges, obstacles, and opportunities you might face. Like astrology, it claims to give you a hint on what can help and what cannot in your life.

HISTORY

Numerology is thousands of years old. In addition, the traces of it lies in Egyptian and Babylonian documents. Pythagoras, the Greek philosopher, is considered as the Father of Numerology. However, the man who gave 'Numerology' its name and recognition is Dr. Julian Stenton.

NUMEROLOGY MEANING

Etymologically numerology is a combination of two words **'numero'** meaning numbers and **'logy'** that stands for logic or science. A numerology horoscope is created on the basis of calculations of the date of birth and letters of a birth name. Each letter in the birth name stands for a particular number.

Each numbers stand for certain alphabetical letters. In numerology, each number has its own significance. They are used to understand the inner traits of a person, his character, goals, his good, and bad phases, his career, relationship, and more.

Each person is associated with multiple numbers in numerology that are calculated in different ways. Each number indicates a certain phase of your personality or future.

MEANING, COMPONENTS, RELEVANCE AND APPLICATION OF NUMEROLOGY

Numerology is a belief system that suggests a connection between numbers and various aspects of human life. It assigns meaning to numbers and uses mathematical calculations to derive insights into a person's personality, life path, and destiny. Here are the key components, relevance, and applications of numerology:

1. **Meaning of Numbers:**
   - Numerology assigns specific meanings to numbers from 1 to 9, as well as to "master numbers" 11, 22, and sometimes 33.
   - Each number is associated with particular traits, characteristics, and energies. For example, the number 1 is often associated with leadership and independence, while 7 is linked to spirituality and introspection.

2. **Core Numbers:**
   - In numerology, several core numbers are calculated from a person's name and birthdate:
   - **Life Path Number:** Derived from the birthdate, it represents one's life journey and overall purpose.

- **Expression (Destiny) Number:** Calculated from the full name, it reflects one's natural talents, strengths, and potential life path.
- **Soul Urge (Heart's Desire) Number:** Also calculated from the full name, it reveals one's inner desires and motivations.
- **Personality Number:** Derived from the consonants in the name, it represents the outer personality that others perceive.

3. **Relevance of Numerology:**
   - **Self-Discovery:** Numerology can be used as a tool for self-discovery, helping individuals gain insights into their own personality, strengths, and challenges.
   - **Relationships:** Numerology is often applied to assess compatibility in relationships, including romantic partnerships and friendships.
   - **Decision-Making:** Some individuals use numerology to make decisions, choose career paths, and understand their life's purpose.
   - **Personal Growth:** Numerology can offer guidance for personal growth and development, helping individuals make positive changes in their lives.
   - **Timing:** Numerology can be used to analyze favorable and challenging periods in a person's life, offering insights into the timing of important decisions or events.

4. **Applications of Numerology:**
   - **Numerology Readings:** Trained numerologists provide personalized numerology readings to

individuals, offering insights into their core numbers and life path.

- **Name Analysis:** Numerology can be used to analyze the influence of a person's name, including its compatibility with their birthdate and its impact on their life.
- **Business and Career:** Some individuals and businesses use numerology to choose auspicious names, dates, and branding strategies.
- **Relationship Compatibility:** Numerology can be applied to assess the compatibility between two individuals based on their core numbers.
- **Event Planning:** Numerology is sometimes used to select auspicious dates for events, weddings, and other significant occasions.

Numerology is often viewed as a form of divination and is not considered a science by the mainstream scientific community. Its interpretations are subjective and can vary among practitioners. The relevance of numerology is a matter of personal belief, and individuals who seek numerology readings or guidance should approach it with an open mind and use it as a tool for self-exploration and personal insight.

THE DIFFERENT INDICATORS IN NUMEROLOGY

Numerology believes in life path number. It is a number that describes you in details. You can find your life path number by adding your birth date.

Suppose, you are born on 3rd April 1995, then add 3+4=7. Now add, birth year, 1+9+9+5 = 24. Add 2 and 4, equals to 6. Add, 7 with 6. The result is 13. Now add 1 and 3 to get a single-digit number. You will get 4. This is your life path number. Besides, people who share the same number have similar characteristics and life pattern.

1. **Life path number:** This is the most critical number in your numerology chart and is calculated using your birth date. It reveals your strengths, weaknesses, challenges, lessons, and events you are likely to face in your lifetime. This number can help you see the path more clearly and spot the opportunities.

2. **Destiny number:** This number is calculated using your first name and surname. It is also known as expression, name or '**Naamank**' number. It gives you a glance of your purpose in life. It describes your character, unveils your goals and gives you an idea on how to achieve them, and also lets you know the obstacles that can come your way.

3. **Personality number:** This number is calculated using the consonants in your first name. It is also known as the dream or inner-dream number. The number describes your personality and gives you an idea of how others see you. Knowing how others perceive you will help you overcome fallacious perceptions and let your inner soul shine through.

4. **Soul number:** This number is calculated using the numbers corresponding the vowels in your first name and surname. It is also known as soul urge number or heart desire number. It gives you an insight of your inner strengths, likes, dislikes, and resources. It says who you

are and reveals the inner self that you may have kept hidden from others.

The numerology most frequently practiced today is based on the teachings of the ancient Greek philosopher – 'PYTHAGORAS'.

Pythagoras was a brilliant mathematician, but he wasn't just interested in quantitative solutions. He believed that the physical world was comprised of the energetic vibrations of numbers, and developed a system that corresponded letters with integers. His practice was a study of numerical interconnectivity.

Just as astrology the planets and zodiac signs are connected to specific attributes within astrology, according to the teachings of numerology, certain numbers are associated with specific traits or themes.

These numbers are used to offer insight on personality, future events, and even life's greater purpose.

But you don't need to be a math person to explore the magic of numerology. All it takes to start uncovering the mystical properties of numbers is a pen, paper, and some simple arithmetic (or the nearest calculator).

Like in Astrology you can predict the results on a yearly, monthly & daily basis (using the Dasha system), the same can be achieved using the Pythagorean system in Numerology and can be linked to planets in Astrology for better understanding. It's a beautiful pragmatic tool for not only Numerologists but also for practicing Psychologists to identify the circumstances of the person, one is passing through & his/her make-up on physical / mental / emotional / spiritual levels.

2

THE PYTHAGOREAN NUMEROLOGY

PYTHAGOREAN NUMEROLOGY

1	2	3	4	5	6	7	8	9
A	B	C	D	E	F	G	H	I
J	K	L	M	N	O	P	Q	R
S	T	U	V	W	X	Y	Z	

1	=	A, J, S
2	=	B, K, T
3	=	C, L, U
4	=	D, M, V
5	=	E, N, W
6	=	F, O, X
7	=	G, P, Y
8	=	H, Q, Z
9	=	I, R

3

NUMBER INTERPRETATIONS

Number 1 (10/1, 19/1)

Just as Aries, the first sign of the zodiac, is about action and initiation, in numerology,

1 is linked to forward motion. 1 symbolizes a pioneering spirit, independent nature, and innate leadership capabilities.

On a bad day, 1 can be a bit bossy or boastful, hiding any insecurities behind over-developed self-importance.

1 must remember that although it is first, it can very quickly become the loneliest number.

Even the most autonomous 1s need the support of their friends, family, and lovers.

Number 2 (11/2, 20/2)

2 is linked to sensitivity, balance, and harmony.

Within numerology, the 2 vibration assumes the role of the mediator, creating harmony by bringing together dissonant forces through compassion, empathy, and kindness.

2 is linked to psychic abilities and intuition, and if this number appears as a Life Path or Destiny Number, the individual will be astute to subtle energy shifts and emotional nuances.

Because 2 is so sensitive, it is very conflict-averse, and can end up feeling under-appreciated or unacknowledged.

2 must avoid seeking external validation and instead, realize that perfect equilibrium needed already exists within.

Number 3 (12/3, 21/3)

Communication is paramount for 3.

Symbolically, 3 represents the output of two joined forces: It is the essence of creation.

3 is highly gifted at expression, seamlessly sharing innovative and pioneering concepts through art, writing, and oration. Your work inspires, motivates, and uplifts others, and 3 finds great joy making others smile.

However, 3 is also known to be quite moody, and if 3 feels misunderstood, may withdraw entirely.

The escapist tendencies of 3 are easily mitigated by practicing peaceful mindfulness: With such an active imagination, it's important for 3 to find moments of quiet to reset, restore, and recharge.

Number 4 (13/4, 22/4, 31/4)

In numerology, 4 has an earthy-energy and is centred around fortifying its roots.

4 adamantly believes in the physical world and knows that investing in a solid infrastructure is necessary for building a lasting legacy.

Practical, hardworking, and responsible, the vibration of the number 4 is focused on creating logical systems that can support scalable growth.

There is a solidity to 4, however, that can quickly devolve into rigidity; 4 must remember that rules are meant to enhance, not inhibit.

It's easy for 4 to become stubborn, so 4 benefits from learning to loosen up and think outside-the-box. 4 will feel liberated and inspired by finding the bravery to take a few bold risks.

Number 5 (14/5, 23/5, 32/5)
Free-thinking, adventurous, and progressive, 5 is defined by freedom.

5 needs to experience the world by engaging its five senses:
For 5, life lessons are acquired through spontaneous acts of bravery.

Akin to Sagittarius energy within astrology, 5 is known for its playful, impulsive, and vivacious spirit. But on the other side, 5 can become restless and impatient.

Since 5 is always seeking discovery, it has a difficult time accepting life's day-to-day responsibilities — including professional and interpersonal commitments.

5 must remember that when it narrows its gaze, it will discover that the most rewarding exploration exists in its own backyard.

Number 6 (15/6, 24/6, 33/6)
6 is recognized for its nurturing, supportive, and empathic nature.

A true healer, 6 has the ability to solve probiem in both the emotional and physical realms, helping others through its straightforward, yet gentle approach.

6 has a strong sense of responsibility, and cares deeply for its friends, family, and lovers.

This number also can easily communicate with children and animals, displaying a soft tenderness and caretaker spirit. But not *everything* needs to be parented, and sometimes 6's protective energy can become domineering and controlling.

To avoid carrying the world on its shoulders, 6 must learn to build trust and understanding for others: Simply put, everyone must follow their own unique path.

Number 7 (16/7, 25/7, 34/7)

The detectives of numerology, 7 is known for its investigative abilities and analytical skills.

Astrologically, the number 7 can be thought of as a blend of Virgo and Scorpio energy:

7 is extremely detail-oriented, but is driven by inner-wisdom as opposed to tangible realities.

7 has a keen eye, and its astute observations fuel a quick-witted, inventive spirit. Because it can quickly find the flaws in almost any system, 7 is a bit of a perfectionist.

7 will often assume fault, so it's important for this number to counterbalance its inherent scepticism with an open mind. Not everything will be fool-proof — but that's what makes life fun.

Number 8 (17/8, 26/8, 35/8)

8 is all about abundance. Within numerology, this number is linked to material wealth and financial success.

Ambitious and goal-oriented, 8 can effortlessly assume leadership positions through its natural magnetism.

8 applies big-picture thinking to broaden its scope, racing up the top of any ladder to reach extraordinary heights. But with great power comes great responsibility: 8 breeds workaholics, and on a bad day, can become excessively controlling and possessive. However, its negative qualities can be lessened by giving back to the community. By using this success to help others, 8 realizes that there is nothing more valuable than contributing to the greater good.

Number 9 (18/9, 27/9, 36/9)

As the final single digit within numerology, 9 connotes an old soul. 9 is no stranger life's ups-and-downs of life — been there, done that.

Accordingly, 9 can effortlessly synthesize large quantities of stimuli, psychically connecting the dots to form a cohesive whole.

The mission for 9 is to reach its highest state of consciousness, and to help others also achieve this spiritual awareness. 9 isn't afraid to transform, and its malleable spirit inspires others to explore their own ranges of motion.

Since 9, in many ways, has transcended the physical plane, it must constantly remember to anchor itself.

9 must learn to balance the abstract with the tangible, ultimately finding its place at the intersection of fantasy and reality.

Master Number 11 (11/2)

Master Number 11 revs up the energy of Number 2; its purpose is to heal the self and others through its elevated psychic abilities.

Often times, Master Number 11's intuitive gifts are a result of extreme life circumstances:

Master Number 11 has no choice but to cultivate extrasensory talents.

Master Number 11 is connected to spiritual enlightenment, awareness, and philosophical balance.

Master Number 22 (22/4)

Master Number 22, often referred to as the Master Builder, expands on the vibrations of Number 4.

Master Number 22 is inspired to create platforms in the physical realm that transcend immediate realities — by fusing the tangible and intangible,

Master Number 22 cultivates a dynamic long-term legacy. Master Number 22's skills are usually a by-product of early childhood instability that fuels innovative thought. Industrious, creative, and dependable.

Master Number 22 is always on a mission to transform.

NUMEROLOGY DIVINATION EXERCISE – CHARACTER ANALYSIS

Before you begin you must find the numbers that are significant to you. Start off by using the number and letter chart below to find the numbers that are relevant in your date of birth and your name.

BIRTH NUMBER

(This is the number that MOTIVATES your life. This is obtained by adding the numbers in your date of birth.

For example, Dave Reynolds date of birth is 22.12.1949

(2+2+1+2+1+9+4 + 9) = 30

(3+0) =3

Birth number = 3.

Your birth number is the number that motivates and moulds you throughout your life and, unlike your name number, no changes can be made here.

NAME NUMBER

The next step is to find your name numbers. Use the following chart to change the letters of your name to their numerical value. Most people consider this their lucky number.

1	2	3	4	5	6	7	8	9
A	B	C	D	E	F	G	H	I
J	K	L	M	N	O	P	Q	R
S	T	U	V	W	X	Y	Z	

FIRST NAME NUMBER

Write your first name and its associated numbers, and add the numbers together as you did for your birth number.

For example:

D	A	V	E
4	1	4	5 = 14

First name number = 5

Here the major influence in the first name Dave is five. Include any other name that you have if it is used in your daily life.

For example, your first names may be Sarah and Jane, and you are addressed as Sarah Jane. My other first name is Elizabeth but it is a name that is never used so I do not consider it when working with numerology.

Your first name displays **the CHARACTER that you show to your friends, those people who address you by no other name than your first name.** Now find the vowels in your first name, enter them in the grid below and add them together until you again have a single digit.

VOWEL NUMBER

For example:

D	A	V	E
	1		5 = 6

The vowels in your first name will show your INNER PERSONALITY. This is the side of your **character or nature that you keep to yourself.**

CONSONANT NUMBER

Now find the consonants in your first name, enter them below and add them together until you again have a single digit.

For example:

D	A	V	E
4		4	= 8

The consonants in your first name will **show the side of your nature that personality that you allow others to see,** your OUTER PERSONALITY.

SURNAME NUMBER

Now repeat this exercise with your surname.

R	E	Y	N	O	L	D	S
9	5	7	5	6	3	4	1
9 +	5 +	7 +	5 +	6 +	3 +	4 +	1 = 40

4 + 0 = 4

WHOLE NAME NUMBER

Now add together your first name number and your surname number only.

Dave Reynolds' first name number is 5 and his surname number is 4, therefore his whole name number is 9.

The whole name number displays the **character that you show to associates** or in situations where you are required to sign your name.

DESTINY NUMBER

The next step is to find your destiny number. Your destiny number is a combination of your name and birth numbers and, as with your name number, changes can occur here through marriage, divorce or choice.

For example:
Birth number: 3
Whole name number: 9

Add the two together until you have a single digit:
3 + 9 = 12
1 + 2 = 3   –   So Dave Reynolds destiny number is 3.

PREDICTION NUMBER

This will show the general indications for any month of any year and must be recalculated each year as your numbers will change from year to year.

To discover your monthly number, you must first take your destiny number and then add the value of the month and year in question.

Each month has its own value and the following table will help you with your calculations.

JAN = 1 **FEB = 2** **MAR = 3**
APR = 4 **MAY = 5** **JUNE = 6**
JULY = 7 **AUG = 8** **SEP = 9**
OCT = 10 **NOV = 11** **DEC = 12**

Example:

To calculate the month of October 2006 for Dave Reynolds the following formula is used:

His destiny number = 3
2006 (2 + 0 + 0 + 6) = 8
This new total is the prediction number =
3 + 1 + 8 = 12
1 + 2 = 3

You can expand on this by adding the entire date, For example, to use the date 25/04/2004 the numbers that you would add together would be:

For the day 2+5=7
For the month = 4
For the year 2004 = (2 + 0 + 0 + 4) = 6
Total = 7+ 4 + 6 = 15 = 1 + 5 = 6

Then Dave would add his destiny number to the number six. 6+3=9.

Now to recap:

Dave's first name number	**5**
Dave's inner personality	**6**
Dave's outer personality	**8**
Dave's full name	**9**
Dave's birth number	**3**
Dave's destiny number	**3**

5

RELATIONSHIP BETWEEN NUMEROLOGY & ASTROLOGY

RELATIONSHIP OF NUMEROLOGY WITH ASTROLOGY

Astrology and Numerology are metaphysical sciences. Therefore, the relationship between numerology and astrology is a close one. Let's first look at the differences:

1. Astrology is the study of the movement of planets and other celestial bodies and their effects on our life, while numerology deals with numbers and names.
2. Numerology talks of vibrating numbers and the energy released by them. On the other hand, astrology doesn't believe in the vibrations of numbers. For them, it is just a tool for calculations.

CONNECTION BETWEEN NUMEROLOGY AND ASTROLOGY

Astrology is not independent of numerology. Numbers are an important part of astrology for reading birth charts and calculating planetary positions. Astrologists make use of calculation based on degrees, angles, distance when explaining different phases of a person's life.

The basic premise of numerology is numerical where each number stands for a particular planet. Besides, it is influenced by the energy released by these planets. Hence, numerologists will assign you a number from 0-9, each having its own planet and zodiac sign.

THE CONNECTION BETWEEN NUMEROLOGY & ASTROLOGY

Both astrology and numerology are considered as science. At the core of science is maths. And maths deals with numbers. Hence, there is a solid bond between both areas of metaphysics.

As astrology talks of groupings according to their zodiac signs, similarly, numerologists believe that vibrating numbers from 0-9, 11, and 22 directly affect your personality. It explains that people with the same number will have similar strengths and weaknesses.

PYTHAGOREAN NUMEROLOGY		
A J S	1	SUN
B K T	2	MOON
C L U	3	JUPITER
D M V	4	RAHU
E N W	5	MERCURY
F O X	6	VENUS
G P Y	7	KETU
H Q Z	8	SATURN
I R	9	MARS

HOW DO NUMEROLOGY & ASTROLOGY WORK TOGETHER

Astrology will explain your birth chart. While, numerology can be used to determine your lucky number, lucky colour, and lucky name. Hence, anyone who makes the best use of the compatibility of numerology and astrology can give you the most accurate predictions.

6

NUMEROLOGY & ITS VARIOUS ASPECTS – (TF)

	1	2
NUMBER	**TRAITS**	**DESCRIPTION**
1. LEADER	Original, independent, courageous ACHIEVER, strength, creative	The number 1 symbolizes the principle of BEGINNING or initiation. It signifies that a person must learn to stand-alone, be assertive, and achieve recognition for his or her talents. Therefore, the 1 is ambitious, an achiever, and fares best when it is allowed to demonstrate its own ideas. It is self-sufficient, inventive, wilful, and dominant. Its energy is masculine, focused, and rational.
2. PARTNER	Diplomat, friend, artist, enduring PEACEMAKER, gentle, insightful, sensitive	The number 2 symbolizes the principle of coming together with another, and is interested in partnership. It signifies that a person is generally supportive, and that issues of intimacy and diplomacy are at work. The 2 is very aware of other's needs as well as its own, and strives to demonstrate friendliness, understanding and tact. It is artistic, shy, thorough, and analytical. Its energy is feminine and magnetic.
3. OPTIMIST	Creative, social, easygoing VISIONARY, humorous, energetic, spontaneous	The number 3 symbolizes the principle of growth. When the initiating force of 1 unites with the germinating energy of 2 there is fruitfulness – 3. It signifies that there is a synthesis present – that imagination and an outpouring of energy is in action. The 3 is optimistic and fun-loving, and strives to uplift and colour its surroundings. Its energy is enlivening, youthful, and enthusiastic.

3	4	5	6	7
GIFTS	**CHALLENGES**	**PERSONAL GOAL**	**FEARS**	**SUCCEDS AS**
Self-sufficiency, invention, mastery	Stubbornness, egotism, bluntness, ambition, dominance, wilfulness, impulsiveness	Establishing individuality; making a name	Being overlooked; not using talents	Writer, director, inventor, president, public figure, business owner, designer
Charm, understanding, supportiveness, loving	Self-consciousness, fear, over-conscientiousness, hesitation	Reciprocal relationships; security	Unknown, unplanned change, being alone, making a mistake	Artist, technician, psychologist, spouse, healer, bookkeeper, coordinator
Enthusiasm, imagination, versatility	Exaggeration, lack of direction, unfinished projects, sensitivity to criticism, laziness	Enjoy life, stay young, play	Loss of youth, restriction, boredom	Motivator, coach, writer, musician, artist, parent, salesperson, communicator/all media

	1	2
NUMBER	**TRAITS**	**DESCRIPTION**
4. PRACTICAL	Application, determination, serious BUILDER, doer, manager, traditional	The number 4 symbolizes the principle of putting ideas into form. It signifies work and productivity. The 4 is constructive, realistic, traditional and cautious. It is the number of system, order, and management.
5. PROGRESS	Freedom, activity, influence ADVENTURER, sensualist, promoter, flair	The number 5 symbolizes the principle of multiplicity, progression, and passion. It signifies the need for change, variety, and new growth. It is the broadcaster – disseminating information and asking questions. It is a public number – outgoing, fast-moving, and mercurial. The 5 is active, daring, non-conventional, unpredictable, and attracted by the physical senses and indulgences. It is pragmatic and opportunistic and very persuasive. It may be undependable.
6. SERVICE	Domestic, responsible, careful TEACHER, conventional, provider, healer	The number 6 symbolizes the principle of nurturing, caring, and harmony. It signifies the need for stability and a solid home-base with comfort. It is the teacher, trainer, and parent. It is happiest in conventional or familiar surroundings opinionated and frugal or anxious when insecure. The 6 is rarely selfish, and may take on the burdens of others unnecessarily. It loves tradition, and is health-oriented.
7. INVESTIGATOR	Specialist, inventor, SPIRITUAL, thoughtful, eccentric, loner	The number 7 symbolizes humanity's deep inner need to find depth, meaning, and spiritual connection. When the creature needs of food, self-expression material and domestic achievements have been met, we turn to the deeper levels of life – to learn, to educate ourselves and to find purpose. The 7 is an investigator, an inventor, and must have solitude in which to find the inner voice. Sevens tend to be different, eccentric, or loners and are very discriminating in all areas.

3	4	5	6	7
GIFTS	**CHALLENGES**	**PERSONAL GOAL**	**FEARS**	**SUCCEDS AS**
Concentration, realistic, values system	Rigidity, too cautious, limited viewpoint	Accomplishment, security	Sudden change, deprivation, loss	Earth scientist, business – owner, developer, lawyer, administrator, office-worker, body worker
Resourceful, magnetic, motivated, competitive	Restlessness, procrastination or activity with no direction, lack of follow through	To win, to experience life to the maximum	Growing old, not seeing the world, boredom	Public figure, developer, speculator, designer, news work, performer, change agent
Caring, ability to compromise, reliability	Anxiety, being over-controlled, co-dependency, guilt	To provide for other's well-being, to create security and harmony, to love and be loved	Lack of resources and love; world going to hell	Parent, educator, caterer/restaurateur, nurse, body worker/health consultant, traditional professional, counsellor, coach
Mental understanding, analysis, perfection	Pride, narrowness, distance, rigidity, connection to the past, argumentative, temper, silence	To maintain control over life; to understand	Failure to achieve standards, making a mistake	Consultant, professor, analyst, earth/maritime occupations, individualist, observer, occultist

NUMBER	1 TRAITS	2 DESCRIPTION
8. POWER	Executive, professional, strength, organiser, money PROBLEM SOLVER, achiever, judgment	The number 8 symbolizes the principle of domination, control, and achievement. It is the executive decision-maker. The 8 tends to be rather formal, stern, and hard-headed. More comfortable in the realm of material, tangible facts, the 8 will be truly exceptional as soon as it develops its spiritual connection and intuition. A natural leader with a good grasp of how to accomplish any goal, it must learn compassion.
9. UNIVERSAL	Generalist, multi-talented, teacher HUMANITARIAN, healer, artist, actor, old-soul	The number 9 symbolizes the principle of a universal philosophy or consciousness. It is the dreamer, and feels at home in the realm of the arts, medicine, religion, drama, and philosophy and metaphysics. It is a healer and educator, acting always for the benefit of others. The 9 looks for solutions from the inspirational, intuitive, and creative worlds. Its energy is loving, compassionate, diffuse, and global.

3	4	5	6	7
GIFTS	**CHALLENGES**	**PERSONAL GOAL**	**FEARS**	**SUCCEDS AS**
Decisiveness, courage, focus, delegation	Belligerence, manipulation, anger, judgment	To exercise control over environment, to achieve power and status	Loss of prestige, being at the mercy of circumstances or of others less capable	Any type of professional, business owner, publisher, contractor, engineer, financial analyst, judge
Understanding, communicating, influencing	Drifting, tolerance, losing focus, bad habits	To make an impact in a big way; expansion	Restriction of any kind, losing control of emotions	Minister, occultist, health/body worker, counselor, artist/ craftsperson, world/ community leader

CHROMOTHERAPY

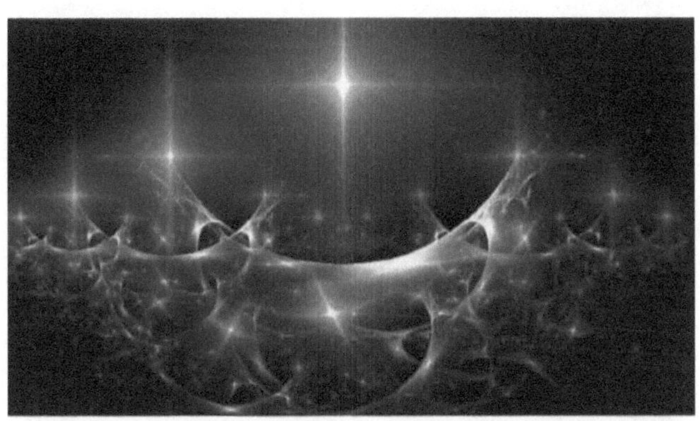

1. **INTRODUCTION OF CHROMOTHERAPY – THE SCIENCE OF COLOURS**
2. **SIGNIFICANCE OF "VIBGYOR" IN CHROMOTHERAPY**
3. **CHROMOTHERAPY: ITS METODOLOGY & BENEFITS**
4. **COLOUR & ITS RELATION WITH 7 CHAKRAS ENERGY SYSTEM**
5. **COLOUR & ITS DIFFERENT CHARACTERISTICS – DAY-WISE – (TF)**

1

INTRODUCTION OF CHROMOTHERAPY – THE SCIENCE OF COLOURS

CHROMOTHERAPY is the science of using colours to adjust body vibrations to frequencies that result in health and harmony.

Humans need the Sun's light, which is broken into seven distinct rays, to live. If there is an imbalance in these colours within our bodies, it can manifest itself in mental or physical distress. Each colour possesses frequencies of a specific vibration, and each vibration is related to different physical symptoms.

Chromotherapy is the use of the visible spectrum, or colour light, to heal the physical, mental and spiritual energy imbalance that tends to lead to disease. It is one of the most holistic and simple methods to cure illness.

This healing modality does not require to consume anything, nor does it require putting anything on your body like an ointment. Simply lay or sit under the desired colour.

Each colour charges our cells a certain way, but it is important to acknowledge that, it imparts a certain amount of energy manifesting as creativity, motivation, happiness, or energy that relaxes our bodies, clears the mind of anxiety and stress, and gives us a good night of rest physically and mentally.

MEANING, COMPONENTS, RELEVANCE AND APPLICATION OF CHROMOTHERAPY

Chromotherapy, also known as colour therapy or colour healing, is a complementary and alternative therapy that involves the use of colours to promote physical, emotional, and spiritual well-being. Here are the key components, relevance, and applications of chromotherapy:

1. **Meaning of Colours:**
   - Chromotherapy is based on the idea that different colours are associated with specific energies, vibrations, and qualities.
   - Each colour is believed to have a unique effect on the body and mind. For example, red is associated with energy and vitality, while blue is linked to calmness and relaxation.

2. **Components of Chromotherapy:**
   - **Colour Selection:** Chromotherapy involves selecting specific colours for various therapeutic purposes. This may include the use of coloured light, coloured fabrics, or coloured surroundings.
   - **Light Sources:** Light therapy is a common form of chromotherapy, where coloured light is directed onto the body or into the environment.
   - **Visualization:** Some forms of chromotherapy involve mental visualization of specific colours to promote healing and balance.

3. **Relevance of Chromotherapy:**
   - **Holistic Healing:** Chromotherapy is often viewed as a holistic healing approach that addresses the

physical, emotional, and spiritual aspects of a person's well-being.

- **Energetic Balancing:** It is believed that colours can help balance the body's energy centres (chakras) and promote overall health.
- **Emotional and Mental Well-Being:** Chromotherapy is used to address emotional and mental health issues, including stress, anxiety, and depression.
- **Physical Health:** Some proponents of chromotherapy use it to address physical ailments and discomforts.

4. **Applications of Chromotherapy:**
   - **Light Therapy:** Coloured lights are applied to specific areas of the body or used in light therapy devices to promote healing and relaxation.
   - **Colour Visualization:** Individuals may engage in guided meditation or visualization exercises that involve focusing on specific colours to promote healing and balance.
   - **Colour Baths:** Some people take colour baths by adding coloured bath salts or coloured lighting to their baths to experience the therapeutic effects of colours.
   - **Colour in Interior Design:** In Architectural and interior design, specific colours are chosen to create environments that promote certain moods and feelings. For example, blue may be used in healthcare settings to create a calming atmosphere.

It's important to note that while chromotherapy is widely used in alternative and holistic health practices, it is not considered a scientifically proven medical treatment. The effectiveness of chromotherapy is often based on anecdotal evidence and personal experiences. Therefore, individuals interested in chromotherapy should approach it as a complementary therapy and consult with qualified practitioners when seeking treatment for specific health concerns.

Chromotherapy is part of a broader field of complementary and alternative medicine (CAM) and is often used in conjunction with other holistic therapies, such as aromatherapy, meditation, and energy healing, to promote overall well-being and balance.

Chromotherapy works on various energy points to help our body re-establish its natural balance. It accomplishes this via the full spectrum of visible light, each colour of which addresses a separate bodily need.

[A pictorial representation of the VIBGYOR colour effects on human beings from the Cosmic source]

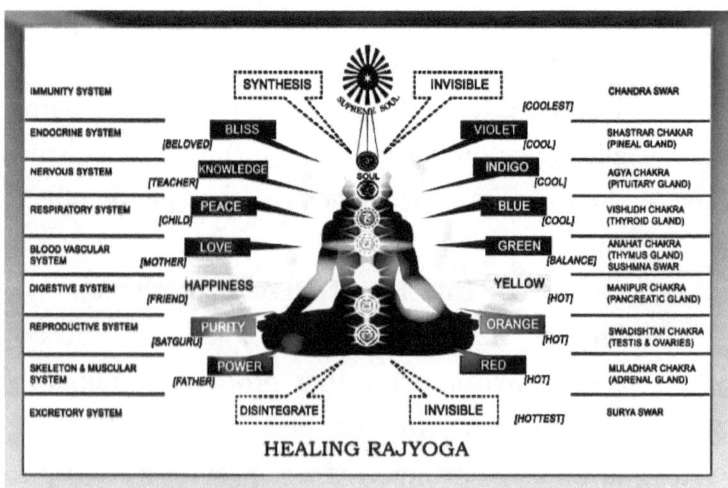

THE SCIENCE OF COLOUR THERAPY – CHROMOTHERAPY

Light is responsible for turning on the brain and the body. Light enters the body through the eyes and skin. When even a single photon of light enters the eye, it lights up the entire brain. This light triggers the hypothalamus, which regulates all life-sustaining bodily functions, the autonomic nervous system, endocrine system, and the pituitary (the body's master gland).

The hypothalamus is also responsible for our body's biological clock. It also sends a message, by way of light, to the pineal organ, which is responsible for releasing one of our most important hormones, melatonin.

The release of melatonin is directly related to light, darkness, colours, and the Earth's electromagnetic field. This necessary hormone affects every cell in the body. It turns on each cell's internal activities, allowing them to harmonize with each other and nature. **The pineal gland is believed to be responsible for our feeling of oneness with the universe and sets the stage for the relationship between our inner being and the environment.**

If that relationship is harmonious, we are healthy, happy, and feel a sense of well-being. An imbalance in this relationship makes itself known in the form of disorders or disease in our physical, mental or emotional states.

The Pineal is our "light meter", and receives information from the heavens above, to give us that sense of oneness with the universe, and from the Earth's electromagnetic field below to keep us grounded. A perfect balance is necessary to maintain our health and to keep us in harmony with the environment.

Colours are all vibratory. Each of the colour photons has its own wavelength and frequency. The body recognizes these waveforms and responds to them. The way we perceive colour is because of the vibration it holds.

THE VISIBLE SPECTRUM OF COLOURS AT DIFFERENT WAVELENGTH

Electromagnetic Radiation	
Infrared > 625 nm	
visible light	**Wavelength (nm)**
Red	625 - 740
Orange	590 - 625
Yellow	565 - 590
Green	520 - 565
Cyan	500 - 520
Blue	435 - 500
Violet	380 - 435
Ultraviolet < 380 nm	

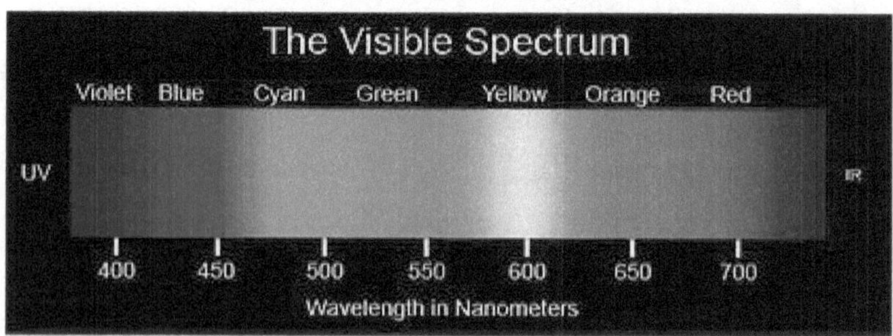

COLOUR & ITS EFFECTS ON HUMAN BEINGS ON THEIR PHYSICAL, MENTAL & EMOTIONAL ENERGY LEVELS AT DIFFERENT WAVELENGTH FREQUENCIES.

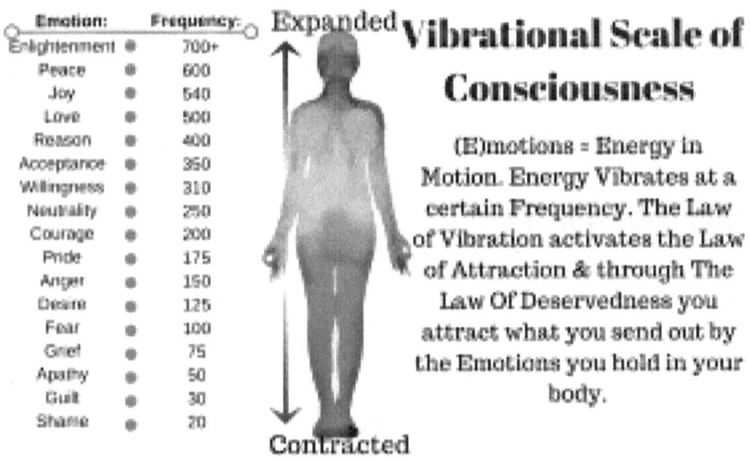

Chromotherapy provides colours to the electromagnetic body or the aura (energy field) around the body, which in turn transfers energy to the physical body. This makes chromotherapy the most effective among various therapies.

Colours have a profound effect on us at all levels—physical, mental and emotional. If our energy levels are blocked or depleted, then our body cannot function properly, and this in turn can lead to a variety of problems at different levels in form discomfort, strain, stress, pain, disorders/diseases.

2

SIGNIFICANCE OF 'VIBGYOR' IN CHROMOTHERAPY

INTRODUCTION

Colours have very important role in our lives and are a great gift by God. Polychromatic light or what we call as white light is composed of seven different colours. However, these colours are split only when passed through a prism and form **VIBGYOR.**

All the colours of VIBGYOR are distinct and useful in their behaviour and character.

These colours have different frequencies that produce magnetic effects on our system due to vibrations. Such magnetic effects produce a feeling of smoothness and relaxation in us.

Our body has composition of different minerals and vitamins that are necessary for us, so has been also said about colours. In fact, all the colours of VIBGYOR are present in a healthier person in perfect balance.

If any how such balance is disturbed, there may be onset of diseases. Hence colours are healers and nourishers of our body that stimulate varied responses on us.

VIBGYOR is an acronym that represents the seven colours of the visible light spectrum in chromotherapy and other colour-related fields. Each letter corresponds to a specific colour:

- **V:** Violet
- **I:** Indigo
- **B:** Blue
- **G:** Green
- **Y:** Yellow
- **O:** Orange
- **R:** Red

THE RELEVANCE OF 'VIBGYOR' IN CHROMOTHERAPY

1. **Representation of the Visible Light Spectrum:**
   - VIBGYOR represents the natural progression of colours in the visible light spectrum. When sunlight or white light passes through a prism or water droplets, it disperses into these seven colours. Each colour has a unique wavelength and energy associated with it.
2. **Chakra Alignment:**
   - In various healing traditions, particularly in the context of Yoga and Ayurveda, VIBGYOR colours are associated with the body's energy centres, known as chakras. Each chakra is linked to a specific colour, starting with violet for the crown chakra and ending with red for the root chakra.
   - Chromotherapy practitioners often use VIBGYOR colours to balance and energize the chakras, aiming to restore physical and emotional well-being.

3. **Healing Properties:**
   - Different colours are believed to have distinct healing properties and effects on the body and mind. For example:
   - Violet is associated with spirituality and intuition.
   - Blue is linked to calmness and communication.
   - Green is related to balance and harmony.
   - Yellow is associated with mental clarity and optimism.
   - Orange is linked to creativity and emotional balance.
   - Red is connected to vitality and physical energy.
   - Chromotherapy involves using these colours to address specific health or emotional issues.

4. **Relevance in Interior Design:**
   - VIBGYOR colours are widely used in interior design to create spaces with specific atmospheres and moods. For instance, warm colours like red and orange are often used in dining areas to stimulate appetite, while cool colors like blue and green are used in bedrooms to promote relaxation.

5. **Symbolism in Art and Culture:**
   - VIBGYOR colours are rich in symbolism and cultural significance. They are often used in art, flags, religious symbols, and rituals to convey various meanings and emotions.

6. **Relevance in Chromotherapy Devices:**
   - Chromotherapy devices, such as colour lamps and light therapy systems, are designed to emit

VIBGYOR colours for therapeutic purposes. These devices are used to direct specific colours onto the body or into the environment to promote well-being and balance.

7. **Holistic Approach:**
   - VIBGYOR represents a holistic approach to healing, recognizing the interconnectedness of physical, emotional, and spiritual aspects of well-being. Chromotherapy practitioners consider how these colours can address imbalances in the body and promote overall health.

It's important to note that while the use of VIBGYOR colours in chromotherapy and other contexts is based on traditional beliefs and practices, it is not universally accepted by the scientific and medical communities. Chromotherapy is considered a complementary and alternative therapy, and its effectiveness varies from person to person. Individuals interested in chromotherapy should consult qualified practitioners and use it in conjunction with conventional medical care when needed.

THE '7' RAYS OF THE RAINBOW COLOUR – 'THE MIRACLE OF COSMIC RAYS ON HUMAN EXISTENCE'

I) VIOLET RAYS

Violet colour brings relaxation and stimulates the flow of subtle energies throughout the psychic centres and the nervous system. Violet colour energy denotes attraction, swiftness, encouragement and affection. It provides Vitamin D.

Violet is the colour with maximum frequency and smallest wavelength in the spectrum. It is immune enhancer and the colour element of air. Air is important in our daily life from every aspect, the most important being the survival of life. If we cease to breathe our death is imminent.

Violet colour is known to create generosity, spirituality, beauty and relaxation. It deepens one's appetite, nourishes brain cells and neurons and boosts immune system to fight against diseases. Violet colour is useful for the treatment of skin ailments and nervous imbalance.

Violet colour can be used all over the body. The vibrations of violet colour are of high spiritual content and it would be a waste of these wonderful vibrations if used below our hips.

Violet light should be confined to the forehead, back and front of the head, front and back of the neck and in concentrated form over the heart and between the shoulder blades for effective healing.

II) INDIGO RAYS

Indigo colour energy stands for unity, honesty and gentleness. It calms nerves and lymphatic systems. Improves stomach disorders, migraine, and cataract. Helps in Soothing effect on the eyes, ears and the nervous system.

Gives vitamin K and controls pituitary glands.

Indigo is the colour of imagination. It always creates in its user a sense of accurate imagination, serenity and understanding. It creates feeling of awareness and intuition. It brings deep sleep and relaxes one.

Indigo colour is known to tighten the skin and increase its tone. It strengthens the thick lymph's of the body and nourishes ligaments, cartilages, bones and appendicular skeleton. Secretory gland and urinary tract problems can be better treated with this colour.

Indigo colour is a great purifier for the bloodstream and is also good for mental problems.

The colour has a freeing and purifying agent.

Indigo is linked with and stimulates the brow chakra (third eye) and controls the pineal gland.

Indigo colour can be of great help in dealing with ailments of ears and eyes.

III) BLUE RAYS

Blue colour energy represents the spiritual aspects of the life and that is an endless process. It has greatest healing power that controls the activity of brain

It gives resistance to body against poison, evil effect, germs and reduces pain etc. It helps the person for higher studies and research work.

The whole universe is filled abundantly with this colour. Look at sky and oceans they are all blue in appearance. In fact, 70 percent of earth's surface is covered by oceans.

Blue is the colour of confidence as it creates mental relaxation, vitality, speaking capabilities and increases confidence. It increases one's hearing power by providing a proper magnetic vibration for sense organs. The colour has been found to be helpful in curing whooping cough, gland and throat problems.

Being bactericidal in nature, the blue colour has been also utilized for the cure of skin ailments and dyslexia. It also boosts one's vascular system (blood circulation) and improves health of nerve sheaths. Weight loss can also be rectified with it.

The colour can be applied from the top of the head to the feet. The colour helps in lowering the high blood pressure and in dealing with nervous breakdown.

Blue colour has high, short and quick vibrations and manifest cold.

Blue colour helps people sleep better. For people with severe insomnia, low voltage dark blue light in the bedroom has proven to be beneficial.

IV) GREEN RAYS

Green colour energy is referred to encourage swiftness and freshness, as it is a nature colour that provides happiness, peace and reduces restlessness. It is said that this colour is beneficial to scientists, lawyers, businessman and salesman.

Green colour is what we love to look at. When you are on picnic spot, on a hill station or in any park you feel calm and quiet, as if all worries and anxieties have lost somewhere.

It is all the power of green as it is a master colour. It nourishes parts of brain, creates hope, calmness and peace. It renews one's inner self and creates a sense of love and rest.

This colour is much effective against fever and typhoid. It can also cure skin problems and ulcer like ailments. The most basic colour used in all healings is green. The colour is always used first and last. No matter what you are treating, it starts and finishes with green colour.

Green colour is also one of the safest colours to use.

The colour can be applied all over oneself and can be concentrated to any part of the body

Green colour is the colour of balance that harmonizes the flow of prana or universal life force, throughout the psychic centres.

V) YELLOW RAYS

Yellow colour energy stands for wisdom, ambition, science, and confidence and helps to improve nervousness, skin problems, digestion system and tiredness. It stimulates the brain, liver, spleen, kidney, memory and gives vitamin A.

Yellow colour is the colour of wisdom. It brings in one cheerfulness, mental clarity and increases concentration.

This colour is helpful to patients with bone marrow, skin and intestine problems.

Diseases of excretory organs including liver and intestine can be cured by this colour. Constipation, night blindness, gall bladder stones, kidney stones and paralysis are some of the diseases that yellow colour helps with.

Yellow colour is also known to help in calcium deposits elimination from the body.

Yellow colour signifies wisdom. Any type of mental issues can be relieved by using yellow colour.

A concentrated beam of yellow light about the size of a tennis ball when applied at the base and the front of the neck, has proven to be valuable for all types of nervous conditions.

VI) ORANGE RAYS

Orange colour energy is a mixture of red and yellow that denotes the colour of Saint. Physically orange is the best stimulant, helping us in times of depression, loneliness, and boredom.

Orange "the Social Colour" is known to create creativity, resourcefulness, social confidence, sociability of feelings and happiness.

It is helpful in increasing oxygen supply to the body parts and removes restlessness, anxiety and depression. It can be also used for hypertension, tuberculosis, anaemia, mental troubles and hiccups treatment.

It has been found to be highly useful in treatment of menstrual cramps and ailments like gout, fever and haemorrhage. It nourishes body fat and lymphatic tissues of the body.

Orange colour can be used on liver, kidney, heart, spleen or any other organ, which promotes good circulation.

People suffering from high blood pressure should not use this colour. The more concentrated the colour, the more effective it will be.

VII) RED RAYS

Red is the colour of power. It has least frequency and longest wavelength. It reaches to the extremities due to its power. It is in fact the colour of pioneering spirit, vitality, ambition, sexuality, alertness and vigour. It can treat constipation, goitre, asthma and obesity. It is known to increase blood flow to organs, remove idiocy and numbness in children.

Nerve inactivity that results in excessive sleep and tiredness can also be treated by this power colour.

This colour can strengthen and provide vitality to muscles of face and tendons.

It also treats anaemia and is highly helpful for female disorders.

Red colour should not be given on the head. But when concentrated on to rheumatic joints, it can be beneficial.

The frequency of red colour is slow and long and has high penetrating properties. It can stimulate the aura to such an extent that circulatory blockages can be cleared.

The infra-red rays should not be given over the reproductive organs of a man or a woman and neither they should be given on liver, kidneys or bladder as it can lead to some damage, if used excessively.

THE COMPONENTS AND ITS USAGE TIME OF 'VIBGYOR' COLORS, IN TREATMENT OF HUMAN DISORDERS / DISEASES

In chromotherapy, different colours of the visible spectrum (VIBGYOR) are believed to have therapeutic properties, and they are used to address various physical, emotional, and mental health issues. The usage time and components involved in chromotherapy can vary based on individual needs, preferences, and the specific condition being treated. Here's a general overview of the components and considerations for using VIBGYOR colours in chromotherapy:

COMPONENTS:

1. **Light Sources:** Chromotherapy often involves the use of coloured light sources. These sources can include colour therapy lamps, LED lights, or natural sunlight filtered through coloured filters.

2. **Colours:** Each colour within VIBGYOR is associated with specific healing properties:
   - **Violet:** Spirituality, intuition, calming the nervous system.
   - **Indigo:** Promoting mental clarity, alleviating headaches.
   - **Blue:** Calming, reducing stress and anxiety, promoting relaxation.
   - **Green:** Balancing, soothing, promoting emotional harmony.
   - **Yellow:** Uplifting, energizing, promoting mental clarity.
   - **Orange:** Stimulating creativity, promoting emotional balance.
   - **Red:** Energizing, improving circulation, stimulating vitality.

3. **Treatment Setting:** Chromotherapy can be administered in various settings, such as therapy rooms, spas, or even at home using colour therapy lamps.

4. **Duration:** The duration of chromotherapy sessions can vary based on individual preferences and the condition being treated. Sessions can last from a few minutes to several hours, depending on the therapeutic goals.

USAGE TIME LIMITS:

The usage time limits for chromotherapy depend on factors such as the individual's tolerance, the specific colour being used, and the condition being treated. Here are some general guidelines:

1. **Start Gradually:** It is often recommended to start with shorter sessions and gradually increase the duration if the individual feels comfortable. This allows the body to adjust to the energy of the colours.

2. **Individual Tolerance:** Some individuals may be more sensitive to certain colours than others. If discomfort or agitation arises during a session, it's advisable to discontinue the treatment and consult a chromotherapy practitioner for guidance.

3. **Condition-Specific:** The duration of chromotherapy can be condition-specific. For example, a person seeking relaxation and stress reduction may benefit from longer sessions with calming colours like blue or green. Conversely, someone using chromotherapy for invigoration and energy enhancement may prefer shorter sessions with stimulating colours like red or yellow.

4. **Consultation with Practitioner:** It's a good practice to consult with a qualified chromotherapy practitioner or therapist who can provide personalized guidance on the duration and frequency of sessions based on the individual's health goals and needs.

5. **Self-Observation:** Individuals using chromotherapy at home should pay attention to their body's response

during and after each session. If they experience any adverse effects or discomfort, they should adjust the duration accordingly.

6. **Consistency:** Consistency in chromotherapy sessions is often emphasized. Regular and consistent use of chromotherapy may yield better results for long-term health and well-being.

It's important to note that while chromotherapy is used by some individuals for complementary health and wellness purposes, it is not a substitute for medical treatment. If someone is dealing with a medical condition, they should consult with a healthcare professional for appropriate diagnosis and treatment. Chromotherapy should be used as a complementary therapy under the guidance of qualified practitioners.

3

CHROMOTHERAPY: BENEFITS & METHODOLOGY

Colour Therapy, or Chromotherapy as it's better known, is an ancient form of healing that was prevalent in Asia, Europe and the Middle East.

It uses a combination of light and colour to treat physical and mental ailments.

Colours have always been known to affect people's behaviour in different ways. Some have a calming effect, while others are known to stimulate both, mental and physical activity.

It may not seem very obvious, but colours play a greater role in our lives than most of us realise.

In fact, colours can be so influential on the human mind and body, that they are even considered to have healing properties.

Colour therapy can be used for treating illnesses and disorders, alleviating pain, addressing emotional and mental conditions, and generally maintaining good health.

Like many other alternative treatments, Colour Therapy has grown in popularity over the years and is one of the most sought-after treatments today. It is making a comeback and is one of the fastest growing sectors in natural health.

COLOURS: ITS EMOTIONAL, MENTAL AND PHYSICAL IMPACT ON OUR BODY

EMOTIONAL IMPACT

BENEFITS OF COLOUR THERAPY

Light is considered to be one of the purest healing forces in the universe. The presence or absence of light can affect the Hypothalamus, Pituitary and Pineal glands. This, in turn, can influence our physical and mental health. We've listed a few of the various benefits that come from using colour therapy:

a. Safe and pain-free so it can be used for children, adults and elderly alike
b. Addresses the physical symptoms of an ailment and also its non-physical origin
c. Balances the Chakras in the body
d. Has a positive influence on not only physical levels but also mental and spiritual levels
e. Helps meditation and relaxation, and can enlighten and transform an individual
f. Eliminates emotional blockages before they can manifest as mental or physical illnesses

Apart from these benefits, colour therapy can improve awareness and help individuals understand the need for including certain colours in their daily lives. It can also help natural healing in a body, enabling overall well-being.

Colour therapy is a safe and effective treatment and can be either be used on its own or alongside another therapy like physiotherapy or traditional medicine. Regardless of how it's used, it is important to understand that the therapy can strongly affect the mind and body. That's why it is vital that individuals seek out a professional colour therapist who is well versed in this area of treatment.

THE METHODOLOGY:

I) COLOR SILK THERAPY

Colour Silk Therapy uses coloured silks on the body, primarily over the chakra centres.

Also being natural fabrics, cotton and wool carry a healing vibration as well, but silk carries the highest frequency vibration of any natural cloth. Because of this, coloured silks have the ability to radiate their signature colour frequency to the physical body and energy field (AURA).

The energy of silk is soft yet potent, allowing one to soak up the colour frequency. One of the beauties of Colour Silks Therapy is that we can place an entire sheet of colour over the entire body, or place a single colour on a particular part of the body.

One of the most popular ways of applying colour directly to the body, is to use coloured silks. These are used to place directly onto the body of the patient. It is not usually necessary for the patient to remove his or her clothes for this.

Any natural fabric i.e., cotton can be used where pure silk is not appropriate.

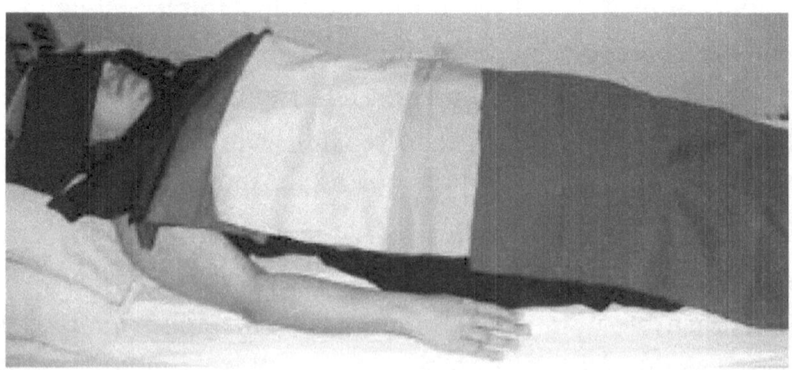

NATURAL PROCESS OF COLOUR HEALING THERAPY BY WRAPPING AROUND COLOURED SILK CLOTHES – METHODOLOGY.

It is accepted that silk is the finest material for the transmission of colour energies to the body, specifically for healing and balancing the body's energies.

- Find a warm, sunny location in your home.
- Play your favourite relaxing music.
- While completely undressed drape a large piece of multi-colored silk over your body and lay down in the sunlight, allowing its rays to penetrate your body through the silk for fifteen to thirty minutes.
- Alternatively, for upper areas of the body, purchase a silk shirt colored to your need. Wear it while relaxing in the sunlight.

(Point of Interest: We all need 10 – 20 minutes of sunshine a day, without sunscreen, to absorb the natural vitamin D from the sun which is essential for calcium absorption by the body)

II) CELLULAR LEVEL HEALING

"Chromotherapy is a narrow band in the cosmic electromagnetic energy spectrum, known to humankind as the visible colour spectrum. It is composed of reds, greens, blues and their combined derivatives, producing the perceivable colours that fall between the ultraviolet and the infrared ranges of energy or vibrations.

These visual colours with their unique wavelength and oscillations, when combined with a light source and selectively applied to impaired organs or life systems, provide the necessary healing energy required by the body. Light affects both the physical and etheric bodies.

Colours generate electrical impulses and magnetic currents or fields of energy that are prime activators of the biochemical and hormonal processes in the human body, the stimulants or sedatives necessary to balance the entire system and its organs."

On a cellular level, once colours penetrate the body, it then detects what your body is lacking (energy, for example), and will aim on feeding your body energy and charging your cells.

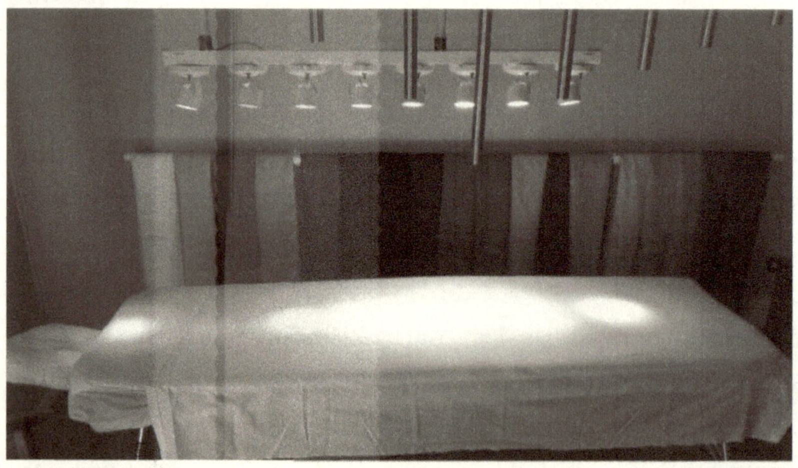

CELLULAR LEVEL HEALING PROCESS BY USING COLOUR LIGHTS TO PENETRATE THROUGH OUR BODY – METHODOLOGY.

Similar to other treatments, Colour therapy begins by diagnosing the underlying cause of the mental or physical issue.

A colour therapist may use counselling as a way to do this during which we could be asked our favourite colours.

A colour therapist also helps you understand the importance of certain colours and how they can impact our daily life in terms of health, healing, inspiration and relaxation.

COLOUR: ITS RELATION WITH 7 CHAKRAS

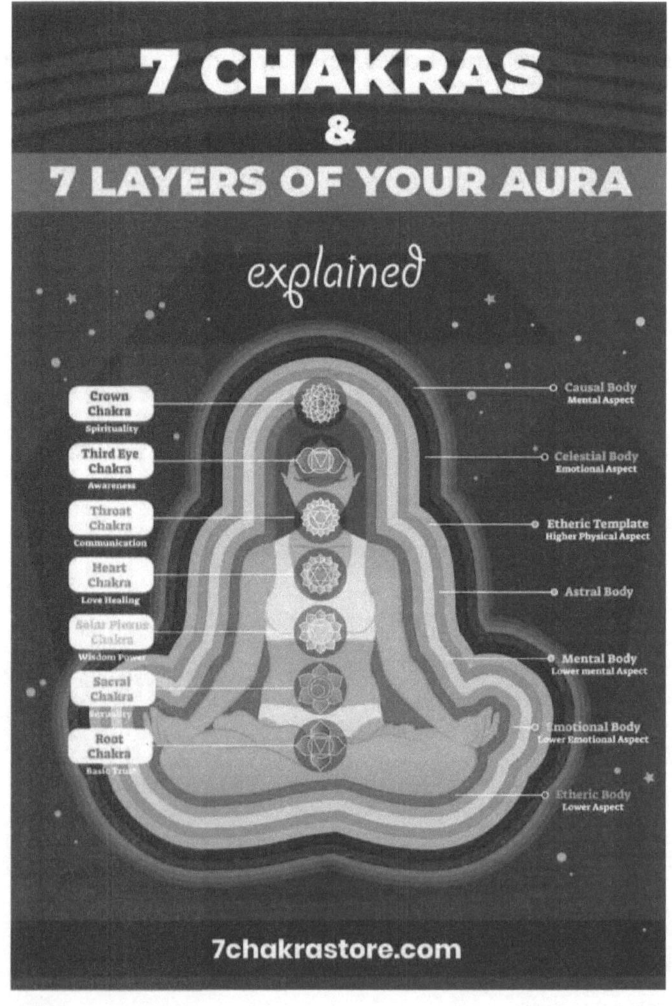

According to Indian philosophy, the chakras are considered the centres of spiritual power and energy within our bodies. There are seven chakras and different colours represent a different chakra: The Chakra system consists of seven energy centres within the human body.

Each of the seven centre points contain energy that regulate the body's functions, from organs, brain, lungs, stomach and so forth, to the immune system, metabolism, and emotions.

Chromotherapy and chakras go hand in hand because each chakra governs a certain colour.

Colours have a type of vibrational energy, which interacts with this magnetic field to treat many disorders. This vibrational energy performs biochemical reactions to revive the energy circulation inside the body.

Today colour therapy is becoming a popular treatment option to cure emotional, physical, and mental patients.

For example, our heart chakra is governed by green. Green's vibration is proven to bring harmony and balance back to one's body while relieving muscle pain.

Green is known to be universally healing, reminding us of the cosmic relationship we share with the universe.

According to Indian philosophy, the body has seven centres of spiritual energy. These are considered to be related to colours which are as follows:

MULADHAR/ROOT CHAKRA – RED COLOUR
It is also called the base cycle. This is the initial cycle of the human body.

The root chakra located at the base of the spine is represented by red colour.

The chakra has to do with our connection with the Earth.

SWADISTHAN/SACRALCHAKRA–ORANGECOLOUR

The sacral chakra, which is 2 or 3 inches below the navel, is represented by orange colour.

This chakra is said to be associated with reproduction, kidneys, adrenals and pleasure.

The chakra is the mind-body chakra.

MANIPURA / SOLAR PLEXUS CHAKRA – YELLOW COLOUR

The location of this chakra is believed to be above the navel and sternum (breast bone).

Its relation is stated in yellow colour. It is positive and associated with well-being.

The solar plexus chakra is associated with liver, pancreas, digestive system, gallbladder, empowerment and well-being.

ANAHATA / HEART CHAKRA – GREEN COLOUR

Its location is near the heart. This cycle is believed to be associated with the heart, lungs, and immunity system and related to green colour.

The colour represents the Heart Chakra. It's associated with heart, lungs and immune system, energy, nervous system, mental focus, compassion and empowerment.

VISHUDDHA / THROAT CHAKRA – BLUE COLOUR

This cycle is located in the throat. It is considered to be related to blue colour.

The chakra is associated with thyroid and metabolism and also with a peaceful expression.

AJNA / THIRD EYE CHAKRA – INDIGO COLOUR (DARK BLUE)

Its location is believed to be between the two eyebrows. It is related to dark blue colour (Indigo).

This cycle is also known as the third eye.

It is related to the pineal and pituitary glands which are associated with our sleep and knowledge.

It influences our sleep cycle, clarity, wisdom, self-esteem and intuition.

SAHASRARA / CROWN CHAKRA – PURPLE COLOUR

It is associated with the Crown Chakra and is located at the top of the head and related to purple colour and considered to be associated with clarity, dreams, spirituality, sleep cycles, dreams, pineal gland and light sensitivity.

5

COLOUR & ITS DIFFERENT CHARACTERISTICS – (TF)

Tabulated Formats of the Colours represented Daywise with its Coressponding Effects Interpretating the Characteristics & Properties.

		1	2	3
SR.	DAY	COLOURS wrt CHAKRA	WAVELENGTH (nm) – UNIT	MENTAL / EMOTIONAL EFFECTS
1	**SUNDAY**	VOILET	380 – 435	Detoxifies, Purifies, Promotes interspecies communication.
2	**MONDAY**	INDIGO	435 – 500	Gives purpose, Inspiration & Protection.

4	5	6	7
PHYSICAL EFFECTS OVER-ALL	**COLOR EFFECTS ON BODY-PART SYSTEMS.**	**COLOUR PROPERTIES**	**COLOUR CHARACTERISTIES**
Strengthen immune systems, Purifies body.	Relaxes the nerves & lymphatic system. Addresses inflammatory & urinary illness.	Stimulates circulation, heart & hameoglobin production; boosts vitality; reduces inflammation & pain;	Gives energy for extracurricular activities; indicates bravery & bold approach; symbolises power, energy, authority & command.
Shrinks tumors, purifies blood, tightens muscles & cleanses the system & aura.	Helps address eye – inflammation, cataract, glaucoma & ocular fatigue.	Assist lung functions; improves digestion, asthma & respiratory conditions.	Reflects spirit of renunciation, gives philosiphical outlook; controls lower nature & enhances concentration of mind. Reflects loving & kindness.

SR.	DAY	1	2	3
		COLOURS wrt CHAKRA	WAVELENGTH (nm) – UNIT	MENTAL / EMOTIONAL EFFECTS
3	**TUESDAY**	BLUE	500 – 520	Calming, Contentment & Confidence.
4	**WEDNESDAY**	GREEN	520 – 565	Peace, Balance & Emotional calm.
5	**THURSDAY**	YELLOW	565 – 590	Mental alertness, Optimism, Playfull.
6	**FRIDAY**	ORANGE	590 – 625	Self confidence, Resilience, Uplifting.
7	**SATURDAY**	RED	625 – 740	Courage, Stimulation, Strength, Groundedness.

4	5	6	7
PHYSICAL EFFECTS OVER-ALL	**COLOR EFFECTS ON BODY-PART SYSTEMS.**	**COLOUR PROPERTIES**	**COLOUR CHARACTERISTIES**
Prevents itching, fights infections, soothes nerves, help skin conditions, burns & cuts.	Stimulates muscles & skin cells, nerves & the circulatory system.	Stimulates circulation, heart & hameoglobin production; boosts vitality; reduces inflammation & pain;	Gives energy for extracurricular activities; indicates bravery & bold approach; symbolises power, energy, authority & command.
Destroys bacteria, rebuilds muscles & tissues, helps infections & injuries.	Provides anti-infectious anti-septic & regenerative stimulation.	Heals & harmonizes; aids in liver functions; stimulates pituitary glands; serves as a germicide.	It signifies metal alertness, prosperity, expansion, academic, sympathetic approach & adoptable nature.
Aids digestion, builds nerves, eliminates worms, helps colic.	Reactivate & purifies skin. Helps with indigestion & bodily stress.	Cleanses, purifies & vitalizes; increases bile flow; bolsters nervous system; serves as antacid; & stimulates the bowl.	Gives optimistic & righteous approach; It denotes strength, wisdom, creative, intelligence, prosperity & charity. Its vibrations are good for fairer sex.
Releases muscle spasms, Strengthens bones & teeth.	Energized & eliminates localized fats. Address Asthama & Bronchitis.	Improves fever and skin problems; cools.	Peacefull & harmonius life; love & affection; artistic & magical pursuits; care for personal image & reputation.
Dissipates radiation, rebuilds the liver, helps laminitis.	Activates the circulatory & nervous systems.	Soothes & balances energy; serves as a motor & cardiac depressant; stimulates the spleen; produces dreaminess.	Colours of peace & tranuility represents noble & divine forces

sanskaaram
The Relevance of
Vedic Science
in Hinduism
A Scientific Approach to
'Rituals'
The ABR Concept
(Act, Belief & Relevance)
CONCEPTUALIZED BY:
Ar. K. SHIVKUMAR

pranayugam
A Wellness and Well-being
Experience Based on Vedic Principles
PUSHPANJALI - The Spiritual Invocation Mantra
DHAYANAM - The Self Realization Mantra
PRANAYOGAM - The 360° Fitness Mantra
The '3' Pillars of Life
'Spiritual, Mental & Physical'
CONCEPTUALIZED BY:
Ar. K. SHIVKUMAR

saptamsidhi
A Vedic Approach to Modern Lifestyle
'A Holistic Concept'
आत्मदीपो भव:
(Be Your Own Light)
CONCEPTUALIZED BY:
Ar. K. SHIVKUMAR

saptamyanam
An Overview of the Universal
Cosmic Energy Effect and its
Implications on Human Existence
An Approach To
'PGR' Measures
(Preventive, Guiding & Remedial)
CONCEPTUALIZED BY:
Ar. K. SHIVKUMAR

aarogyaveda
The Vedic and Contemporary
Holistic Health Approach
for Lifestyle Disorders
An Evaluation of
'PST' Measure
(Prevention, Screening & Treatment)
CONCEPTUALIZED BY:
Ar. K. SHIVKUMAR